Treasures by the Sea

The Golden Isles

The Deluxe Edition

By Jim Jensen

MICKI AND SAMMY
FATHER GOD, THANK YOU FOR MICKI
FOR SAMMY, FOR FAMILY AND FOR
WHAT THEY BRING TO YOUR TABLE.
BLESSINGS.

"LOVE JOY PEACE,..."   GALATIANS 5:22

Jim

Daily Devotionals

East Beach

Saint Simons Island, Georgia

To my family: Barbara. Jenny, John Charles, Johnny, Courtnay, Jamey, Amy, Miguel, Jensy, Isabel, Joy, and Ford.

In Appreciation

"What's next, Lord?" This book is in response to that question. Many of you have asked the same question. So I begin by giving thanks to the dear Lord for the question and for the direction and guidance given.

I was blessed to have been placed in a home where the Lord was honored; a place where love and encouragement lived. My mom, dad, and grandparents pointed us in very clear directions and my extended family did as well. Again, thank you dear Lord.

My brothers and their spouses have been encouragers in life and in the writing of this book. I give thanks again.

So many have given encouragement to this man and to his family. The list seems endless. Through the people of those churches we were honored to serve, we have seen the salt of the earth and the light shining in the darkness. We have given thanks and give thanks.

In these times, God has provided those who have come in from different doors: Bob and Barbara Golding, Jimmy Beasley, Dr. Dave Kranc, Dr. Lana Skelton, Carol Conner, Margot Howard, Leonard and Sally Mann, Robert Conner, Bill Pickard and the list goes on. Thank you.

In January of 2016 on a cruise in the Eastern Caribbean, He continued to provide. Jim Cook and Millie Adams are authors; one is a friend whom I have known for years and the other became a friend on that cruise. Both of them, gifts of God, offered words of encouragement and opened new doors for me.

Moving deeper into 2016, Barbara Golding added new insights into the world of publishing and again opened some new doors and offered strong encouragement. Earlier Robert Conner came into the equation bringing graphic design skills and knowledge about computers. We have spent hours together moving toward the goal. God provides. Thank you for you and for your labor of love.

Finally and most importantly, to the young woman who said yes to me fifty-five years ago, my bride, Barbara Lewis Jensen. I give thanks for her, for her patience, for her love and for her encouragement through the years and especially during the process of writing, Treasures by the Sea. Our three girls and their families have been on the encouragement team all along in many and varied ways. Thank you!

Forward

"And God said, 'Let there be lights in the expanse of the sky to separate the day from the night, and let them serve as signs to mark seasons and days and years'...."

– Genesis 1:14 (NIV)

NO SIGNS!

Another magnificent sunrise, but there will be no bi-plane pulling a flowing sign behind it announcing, "This sunrise today is provided by God for your viewing pleasure." Or a host of heavenly angels, in chorus, announcing in perfect harmony, "Another glorious sunset provided for you by the Maker of the universe and the Redeemer of souls." There will be no sign posted reading, "A gift from the Creator of the planet Earth" by the beach, by the marsh, or even by those beautiful aged live oak trees. On that special sand dollar collected on the beach years ago, there will be no tiny message embedded, "made by God." A visit to a local Coastal Hospital's Nursery you will find no sign on the door reading, "New Arrivals from Heaven, complements of the Lord of Life and the Giver of Joy! Treat with tender love and care." In the stars and moon, there will be no fireworks, or message in the night proclaiming, "A gift from God, for your evening pleasure."

Signs are there like day and night, but they cannot be seen with the naked eye. How then can they be seen? They can only be seen with the spiritual eye. The Lord Jesus put it this way, "And I will ask the Father, and He will give you another Counselor to be with you forever - the Spirit of

Truth. The world cannot accept Him, because it neither sees Him nor knows Him. But you know Him, for He lives with you and will be in you."

Hopefully and prayerfully, these coastal devotionals by God's grace will inspire those who read them to re-examine their own spiritual eye, to strengthen that eye, to rejoice in it or to simply exercise it for the very first time.

Look for the signs! They are everywhere! It will truly make a difference and be a blessing. Good sign hunting!

"The Lord, bless you and keep you: The Lord make his face to shine upon you and be gracious unto you: The Lord lift up his countenance upon you and give you peace."

Table of Contents

Week Eight

Week Nine

Week Ten

Week One

"Two are better than one..., if one falls down, his friend can help him up..., also, if two lie down together, they will keep warm..., a chord of three strands is not quickly broken."

– Ecclesiastes 4:9-12 (selected verses) (NIV)

Trust Me

"Be strong and courageous. Do not be terrified; do not be discouraged for the Lord your God will be with you, wherever you go." – Joshua 1:9 (NIV)

It was indeed a treasure by the sea; a father and son on the beach. I saw the father, by his action, encouraging trust. He was pulling his son on a bogie board over smooth sand and a layer of water. The bogie board was gliding across water and sand with ease. They were having a blast. It was a Kodak moment. The son looked to be about four. He was on his hands and knees on the board. With silent love, his father was saying, "Trust me!"

From that observation, I could already see in my mind's eye that young boy skim boarding. See him tossing the board, hopping on it, staying low, leaning forward, keeping balance and gliding freely. True skimmers do create moving art forms on the beach. It all begins with trust. I could also hear by his father's action, "You can do it!"

I believe we all have had hand and knee experiences, where we have felt totally incapable of standing. Then someone just like this father says with loving action, "You can do it...do not be discouraged...trust me!"

I remember as a young college student a "hand and knee" moment, not my first or my last. She asked me to teach a group of fifth and sixth grade boys in Sunday school. Her name was Mary Worthy. I couldn't say no to her, or to Him (God), but I was on my "hands and knees," like

11

the young boy on the beach. The two of them, God and Mary pulled me along with their steady action of loving care saying, "Trust us. You can do it."

I will in the future have more "hand and knee" moments. You will too. But at this moment, I am skimming. I'm standing up, not alone. With love, joy, peace and hope, I am offering what I have been given so freely. "Yes!"

And Jesus says, "Let not your hearts be troubled, neither let them be afraid."

Lord God, thank you for your promise to be with us. Jesus, thank you for those words, "Father, into your hands I commit my spirit!" Spirit of God, empower us to do the same and put our trust in you. In His holy name. Amen.

Listening for Silence

"But the Lord is in his holy temple; let all the earth be silent before him." – Habakkuk 2:20 (NIV)

Listening for silence..., it happens, but it demands being fully attentive.

It was a beautiful spring morning, the humidity was low and the temperature was in the seventies...another "Chamber of Commerce" day in the Golden Isles. There was a gentle breeze coming out of the southwest. The marsh was in its full glory. It was a perfect moment to listen for silence. "Let all the earth be silent." The choice was made. Distractions like planes, cars, trucks and trailers, all producers of noise pollution, were disregarded. Even the community of various birds that inhabit the edges of the marsh and lift musical notes together, were all gently set aside. Other wonderful alternatives were quickly retired. Even sounds of the gentle breeze were left behind. The focus was set!

Silence came, like it has before, like it will again. It refreshes and renews. It is a place of peace and comfort. It invigorates the spirit and the soul. It happens in communities, in homes, in work places, in schools, in churches, in hospitals, in nursing homes, on battlefields, in prisons, in His great outdoors, and more. This is His world, His temple and He is forever present. Where can I hide from Him? Elijah experiences Him speaking in a gentle whisper. God Himself expresses it through David in this way, "Be still and know that I am God." Isaiah puts it this way, "Those who wait on the Lord will renew their strength. They will soar on wings like eagles; they will run and not be weary, they will walk and not faint." Jesus says, "I will not leave you comfortless, peace, I leave with you, my peace I give unto you, wait until you have received power."

His holy silence continues to give power, purpose, peace, love, joy, hope, and much more. He gives complete and ultimate freedom. There are divine moments of listening and knowing His holy presence. There are choices to be made, moment by moment, day by day. "Let all the earth be silent."

Father God, thank you for the gift of holy silence. Lord Jesus, thank you for those who came before us and encouraged us to listen for silence, to wait and to "be still and to know." Thank you for peace that endures and lives on forever and ever. In the name of the one who still calls His loved ones "to be silent before Him." Amen.

Go Deeper

"Wash me, and I will be whiter than snow." "Create in me a clean heart, O God, and put a new and right spirit in me." – Psalm 51: 7b, 10 (RSV)

It was a quiet Sunday morning. The beach was empty. The tide was out. I whispered, "Lord, speak for your servant is listening."

I walked by the water's edge. No more than fifteen feet from me, I saw the "snakebird". Some know him as the "American Darter." His biological name is Anhinga. I named him the "swimmer" on that day.

His head and long neck popped up out of the deep. In an instant, he returned to the depths. Snakebirds swim underwater. They stay down for long periods of time. They are good fishermen. They make their catch underwater. Another unique thing about the swimmer is that his feather gets wet and must be dried out from time to time by the wind and/or the sun. Water normally rolls off the feathers of waterfowl like a duck, but not so with the swimmer.

The living Lord, through the swimmer, on this day reminded me afresh that I need to go deeper. We were designed for deeper. We were given the need within to listen...to wait...yes...and to be still. We were given the need to immerse ourselves in God's tenderness and mercy daily. We need communion, day by day.

Remember Peter's response when Jesus said He was going

to wash his feet? I need to claim Peter's response for myself, "Lord, not just my feet, but also my hands and my head!"

A disciple of Christ goes deeper. He or she listens..., waits..., and is still. A follower of the Lamb of God allows Him to do what He desires to do with His tenderness and mercy.

"Wash me, Lord, and I will be whiter than snow!"

Lord God, we thank you for your desire to wash and to make us clean. Father, we are tempted not to go deeper... not to listen...not to wait...not to be still. Lord Jesus, help us to be immersed again with your tenderness and mercy, day by day by day. In the name of the one who desires to wash whiter than snow. Amen.

Walking with Dolphins

"Even though I walk through the valley of the shadow of death, I will fear no evil, for you are with me...."
– Psalm 23:4 (NIV)

"Describe a place of relaxation, comfort, peace." Her response was immediate, "Walking on East Beach with dolphins!" "Walking dolphins?" There was laughter, hers included. She went on to say, "You know what I meant." We did. I have walked with dolphins a number of times.

There was not a cloud in the sky. A gentle breeze came out of the south, another "Chamber of Commerce" day! We were walking on East Beach at the edge of the water. No more than thirty yards out dolphins were swimming, (walking), beside us. They were moving through the water slowly and gracefully, as in step with us. When we made our turn to go back up the beach, they also made their turn and stayed with us. It was a treasured moment.

The boy who was a shepherd, became the Shepherd King. He was King David. He walked in "the valley of the shadow of death," but he also understood walking with another. David concluded with a Pre-Easter affirmation for me and for you. Listen again to the Shepherd King, "and I will dwell in the house of the Lord forever."

Mary walked with Jesus and talked with him. She listened. She experienced His grace and His mercy. Mary felt His healing touch. Tears of grief and sorrow flowed. Her heart was broken. Early in the morning, walking "through the

17

valley of the shadow of death," she made her way to the tomb. Mary came to a stranger. He spoke softly, "Mary." At that moment, she understood. Then she ran. She never again walked alone.

It is a treasured moment when dolphins "walk" with us. But it is a sacramental and a divine moment when Jesus walks with us. Mary affirmed it. Peter, James, and John affirmed it. We have too!

Father God, thank you for your love and mercy. We thank you for your desire to walk with us, even "in the valley of the shadow of death." Lord Jesus, thank you for that eternal and divine moment when we recognize that you walk with us day by day, moment by moment. Empower each of us to share what we have so freely received. In the name of Jesus Christ. Amen.

Walking with Dolphins just north of Massengale Park.

Being

"And the secret is simply this: Christ in you! Yes, Christ in you bringing with him the hope of all the glorious things to come." – Colossians 1:27 (JBP)

The sky was blue. The clouds were sunlit. The sandy beach was at its very best. The tide was going out. There was a gentle breeze coming out of the south. Two fishermen prepared their rigs. My bride of fifty-plus years called out, "Hope you have a great day fishing!"

The older fisherman looked around, surveyed his surroundings, and responded, "It's already a great day! Just being here is enough."

What a wonderful affirmation. We felt an instant kinship. "This is the day, the Lord has made. Let us rejoice and be glad in it."

Jesus asked for His Father's blessings, broke the loaf of bread and eyes were opened. They shared with each other how their hearts were strangely warmed. Being with Jesus was enough. No, it was everything!

"Being with the living Lord is everything!" That's Peter's affirmation by the Sea of Galilee. "Lord, you know everything! You know my heart! You know I love you!" Paul affirms, "I count everything as loss for the sake of my relationship with you."

John Wesley, the father of Methodism, affirms these

Biblical truths and finds that his heart was "strangely warmed," because being with Jesus is everything.

As a young boy in a hospital in Texas, I first experienced Jesus being with me and what it means. Being with Jesus is everything!

Hope you have a great day…being with Jesus!
"Rejoice in the Lord, always!"

Father God, thank you for the gift of this day, for the gift of being with you. Lord Jesus, thank you for warming hearts. Warm ours. Empower us to be open and sensitive to your being in our midst. May we by grace share what we have so freely received. In the name of the one who is present. Amen.

Be Secure

"You are the Christ, the Son of the living God!"
– Matthew 16:16 (NIV)

She slowly moved through the sound making her way to open seas. She rode high. She was empty. Her cargo had been delivered. This ship was one of the largest to enter our port. She had fourteen decks, her capacity 5,000 automobiles. We have seen her sister ships moving through the sound, out to open seas many times.

Each automobile needs to be secure. Often on the open sea, storms and troubled waters occur. Ships are tossed to and fro. Vehicles are made secure by nylon lashings. If one automobile is not secure, it will do damage to itself and to those about it. And so it is with human kind. If we are not secure, we will do damage to ourselves and to those about us. Storms and troubled waters occur.

It's an admirable thing, seeking to be secure. We do it in many ways. A mother places a helmet on her young son, as he mounts his bicycle for the first time. Her hope is that he will be safe and secure. It's an admirable thing to be concerned about good health practices. Seven heart bypasses got my attention. I seek to be more secure with diet and exercise. In our personal relationships, we seek to be secure. We search for relationships that are loving, caring, enduring, warm, peaceful, valued, treasured, and precious. Yes, also in personal finances, we seek to be secure. Rightly so. Often when the storms of life are raging, and they do, we lose our security and often do damage to ourselves and to those about us.

Peter understood about doing damage to himself, to others and to Jesus. Remember his words, "I don't know him!" He struggled just as we do. But please also listen to these words, "You are the Christ, the Son of the living God!" Jesus replied, "Blessed are you, Simon, son of Jonah, for this was not revealed by man, but by my Father in heaven." Peter would later be found to be very sure and very secure in his relationship with the Lord of life.

Eternal Father, we thank you for the God-given need you placed in each of us to be secure. Lord Jesus, we thank you for the loving and enduring relationship you offer us that makes us free and secure. Empower us to choose daily Peter's affirmation and to exercise disciplines that will keep us in your will and in your hands. Deliver us from doing harm to ourselves and to others. In the name of the Father, and of the Son, and of the Holy Spirit. Amen.

An empty auto carrier exits the St. Simons Sound at eventide.

Back to Back

"Two are better than one..., if one falls down, his friend can help him up..., also, if two lie down together, they will keep warm.., a chord of three strands is not quickly broken."
– Ecclesiastes 4:9-12 (selected verses) (NIV)

It was early morning. The tide was out. There were blue skies, no clouds, another cool morning on East Beach. It was a new sighting, never seen by these eyes. The couple seemed to be early retirees. They were seated back to back, shoulder to shoulder on a slight rise. Physically, he had her back covered. She was protected and vice versa; she had his back and he was protected. "Two are better than one."

Cardy learned quickly, about "back to back living" abroad a cruiser in the Pacific during World War II. He met the love of his life, Dottie and for over sixty years, they lived that life together. He had her back and vice versa. They were blessed with three precious daughters. This dad always had his girls' backs and continues in that effort today. He learned the lesson in those early formative days. Now his girls are living out "back to back living" with their dad. They have his back. He knows it. That's God's plan. That's the way it is designed to work. It's a beautiful thing to see and to be a part of "back to back living." It's holy and sacramental.

It doesn't always work out that way, but that is God's plan. There is always grief, sorrow, heartache, and pain when it doesn't. Trust me on this!

"A chord of three strands is not quickly broken." For me personally, the third strand is a living and loving relationship with our Father in heaven. He has our back. He never gives up on us. The psalmist puts it this way, "Even though I walk through the valley of death, I will fear no evil, for you are with me!" Jesus says, "I will not leave you as orphans; I will come to you." Our part is to have His back and know the joy of that kind of living. We are to love God with hearts and souls and love our neighbors as ourselves.

May it be said of us, "They had His back!"

Thank you dear Father for having our back, for the eternal gift of "back to back living." Thank you Lord for those you have sent on our path, who had and have our back today. Thank you for the freedom and the joy we have, to choose "back to back living." In the name of the Father, the Son and the Holy Spirit. Amen.

Week Two

"Finally, brothers, whatever is true, whatever is noble, whatever is right, whatever is pure, whatever is lovely, whatever is admirable—if anything is excellent or praiseworthy—think about such things."
– Philippians 4:8 (NIV)

R & R

"My heart is in anguish within me; the terrors of death have fallen upon me, Fear and trembling come upon me, and horror overwhelms me. And I say, "O that I had wings like a dove! I would fly away and be at rest...."
– Psalm 55:4-6 (RSV)

The pelican spoke. I watched her and her friends gathered on the beach for rest and relaxation at the water's edge. They enjoy sand bars. They value that bit of separation. I have seen her being lifted by the ones in front of that straight line formation; gliding so gracefully. I have watched her turn that lanky body into a deep dive; seeking and finding needed food. I have seen her skim just above the water; fearful for her that she might be dashed by an unexpected wave, but she is a very gifted flyer.

It was a magnificent sun-soaked beach. It was July and very hot. The beach was filled with brothers and sisters in much need of R & R. There were those who were taking in the rays. Some were reading. A few were sleeping. Others were simply enjoying the water. A few sandcastles were under construction. Little ones were experiencing the joys of beach life for the very first time. That moment was holy and a precious sight.

I saw my pelican friend beginning to soar. She had found a thermal; a rising current of warm air. The thermal lifted her upward. Around and around she went; higher and higher, almost out of sight. My friend was in the midst of her own personal R & R; being lifted gently by the warm winds of

God. It was another holy sighting.

From time to time, we all need R & R! It's hard to find a bit of separation. There are times when it is difficult dealing honestly with all that comes down the pike. We need time apart. We need brothers and sisters, who join us in that straight line formation. We need to be open to those who offer support, love and care. Lord, daily remind us that we need others. We also need to be ready for those spiritual thermals, when the spirit of the living Lord lifts our souls upward.

Father, thank you for the need for rest. Thank you for spiritual thermals that lift us upward. Thank you for brothers and sisters, who offer us care in your name. Lord, empower us to soar and to be at rest. In the name of the one who offers care and makes thermals and soaring possible. Amen.

Catching a thermal near the Coastal Cottages on a hot summer day.

Higher and higher and higher.

Indispensable

"He took him outside and said, "Look up at the heavens and count the stars - if indeed you can count them." Then he said to him, "So shall your off spring be."
– Genesis 15:5 (NIV)

Walking the beach is more often than not, a quiet experience, except for wind and surf. They can be tuned out easily. The sand tends to muffle and absorb the human step. It was a great day for walking in quietness with the wind and surf tuned out. Then it happened, "Crunch, crunch, - crunch." I had inadvertently walked into a bed of tiny shells. Beachcombers know the sound. It was indeed, one of those serendipitous moments, unplanned and unanticipated but welcomed. I was carried down a fresh spiritual path.

There are millions upon millions of shells on our beach. Some of them are easily seen by the naked eye. Others are not. Only through magnification can they be seen. Each is indispensable in the life of a living beach. We are blessed with a living and healthy beach.

Who has not questioned value and worth? Who has not known denials, fears, doubts, and questionings?

The Father of Nations did. Abram questioned his value and his worth. He shared his fears, his doubts, and questionings with the Lord. The Lord God took him outside and said, "Count the stars... so shall your off spring be." Indispensable.

Jesus understood about questionings. Listening to His followers, he gave this response with love, "Indeed, the very hairs of your head are all numbered. Don't be afraid; you are worth more than many sparrows." Again, indispensable!

The next time you hear, "Crunch, crunch" on your "beach." Look down at the "shells" and remember what you are worth in God's eye. Indispensable. Then give Him thanks again.

Thank you, Father, for the stars in the night sky. Thank you for the shells on the beach. Thank you for your understanding of value and worth. Thank you, Lord Jesus, for your sacrifice and life eternal. Grant that we might never forget that we have been purchased with love and are indispensable. In His holy name. Amen.

Low tide, noontide and treasures of tiny shells, thousands.

Goodness

"But the fruit of the Spirit is love, joy, peace, patience, kindness, goodness, faithfulness, gentleness, and self-control. Against such things there is no law."
– Galatians 5:22 (NIV)

It was one of the first days of autumn; an October afternoon and, another "Chamber of Commerce" day. The temperature and the humidity were low, with blue skies and a gentle breeze. It was an unusual sighting, a family of five; three people and two dogs. They were approaching slowly. The young mom had a back pack with a little baby girl safely tucked in. She was just five months old. She was decked out with a hat and sunglasses and cute as a button. The father was pulling a big red wagon carrying a Weimaraner, a beautiful dog with his ears flopping in the wind. He was a big heavy dog. He was enjoying the beach with his family. There was a smaller dog running back and forth with great gusto.

The dad had just taken a photograph of his wife and their little girl. As I walked by, I offered to take one of the whole family. They were pleased. The new mom was smiling from ear to ear with her little girl in her back pack. The dad reached down, lifted up the smaller dog lovingly and with care. After a couple of shots and returning his phone, I asked the question, "Why was the Weimaraner not running with his buddy?" They showed me a big knot on his left front leg. And then, they shared the bomb shell. "He has been diagnosed with cancer and is in the middle of his treatments so he wears out easily."

They were from Indiana, on vacation in the Golden Isles… first-timers. I saw gentleness, kindness, patience, faithfulness and goodness. I experienced love, joy and peace.

That day, I had not shown those qualities. I had not been patient, kind, gentle, or good. I had missed the love, the joy and the peace. The dear Lord got my attention through a young family from Indiana. Has He ever gotten your attention? I received the message and began plans to make amends!

Thank you, dear Lord, for sending messengers our way. Thank you for never giving up on us. Empower us to be open to your messengers and to the fruit of your Spirit. Forgive us when we fail you. Dear Jesus, may we be bearers of the fruit of your Spirit today. With love, and joy and peace. In His holy name. Amen.

A Toddler's Beach Day

"This is my body given for you, do this in remembrance of me." – Luke 22:19 (NIV)

East Beach was filled with toddlers. They were everywhere. Clearly this was a toddler's beach day. Moms and dads, sisters and brothers, aunts and uncles, grandmothers and grandfathers, friends and loved ones were keeping watchful eyes on their precious toddlers. The toddlers were exploring new territory. Sand was being formed into castles. Surf was being tested with little toes and small baby steps. All of the aforementioned caregivers were often found being helpful with explorations, with constructions, and even with tests. A dad was helping with a sandcastle construction. A mom was using her iPhone to catch memory moments. A big sister was holding a little hand at the water's edge with encouragement. A grandmother was out in the water encouraging her little toddler, just to come in a little deeper. Her words were reassuring, "Don't forget, I am here."

I remember a little toddler on one of her first days at the beach. She had explored, built and tested. She had found it all to be wonderful and very good. She was in the water having fun. My daughter said to her mother, "Don't you know the little fishes are having fun?" A memory was made that day that is still alive.

The beach is a wonderful place for making beautiful memories. Remember those who were intentional on our paths in making memories. Be assured that on East Beach in the early spring, memory-making took place.

On another day and another time, "He took bread, gave thanks and broke it, and gave it to them, saying, 'This is my body given for you; do this in remembrance of me.' " He made a memory that evening, so long ago that changed the world forever. It changed my life, my family's life, you and yours as well. And He still says, "Don't forget, I am here!" He is still making memories. There are those in our midst who will not forget. Never! Millions across this tiny globe still gather together and receive the bread, remembering and celebrating His victory and ours.

Dear Father, thank you for the beach and for beaches everywhere. Thank you for toddlers and for families, who recognize a God-given need to make precious memories. Dear Lord, thank you for taking the bread, giving thanks, breaking the bread and saying, "Do this, in remembrance of me." Dear Jesus, thank you for making memories in our lives that indeed are everlasting. Amen and Amen.

Grace in Action

"But while he was yet at a distance, his father saw him and had compassion, and ran and embraced him and kissed him." – Luke 15:20b (RSV)

Walking on the beach one day, I saw grace in action and also one of God's angels. She was a little girl, a toddler. She had pretty blonde hair. I didn't see her eyes, but I guessed they were blue. She walked, but had not been walking long. The sand made walking more difficult. Still she was up to the challenge. Most likely, it was her first time on the beach. Her mom and her dad were clearly enjoying the moment.

Human beings have natural fears. For some, the sounds of the beach can bring out those fears. For others, the constantly moving water can do the same. I have seen little ones running from the water, filled with fear. There is just too much to take in. Fear rules!

Now for grace in action, the little girl's daddy began playing a toddler's version of red light, green light. With hand motions, he stopped her in her tracks and or moved her forward, "Stop. Go." The little angel stopped and moved as she was directed by her father. She was on cue. He was at the water's edge. When she got to her daddy, he picked her up and moved her back from the water. They did this over and over until finally, he went out into the water with all that fearful sound and movement. Still playing the game, he carefully led her forward right out into the water and into his arms. Without any fear, she followed him. She was with her daddy, having fun, experiencing grace in action.

Thinking back through my life, that has been my grace experience. My dad was there. To be truthful, I was not always on cue like the toddler. I thought I knew what I needed and I didn't need help from anyone. My heavenly Father was always there. Both of my fathers offered loving directions, "Stop. Go." Still, both waited with grace.

Dear Lord, thank you for you. Thank you for not giving up on us, for your patience and faithfulness. Father, thank you for holy truth, "For by grace you have been saved through grace, and this is not your doing, it is the gift of God." Empower us dear Lord to move past fears and doubts and offer grace in action, whenever and wherever we can. Lord, give us wisdom and give us direction. In the name of the one who offers grace in action every moment of every day. Amen.

Walking the High Tide Line

"Finally, brothers, whatever is true, whatever is noble, whatever is right, whatever is pure, whatever is lovely, whatever is admirable—if anything is excellent or praiseworthy—think about such things."
– Philippians 4:8 (NIV)

Walking the high tide line almost always offers treasures… whelks, netted olives, shark eyes, clams, green jackknife clams, cockles, angel wings and the list goes on; treasures from the shell family. Add to those treasures, driftwood in different shapes and sizes; perfect for a desk, a great room, a patio, or a yard. On occasion, sand dollars add to the treasures, but again the list goes on.

Walking the high faith line with the Lord and His followers always offers treasures in abundance. His words are very clear, "I came that they may have life, and have it abundantly." Through faith in Him, treasures are found in abundance. Love, mercy, grace, forgiveness, assurance, new beginnings, second changes, life, hope, new strength, peace, joy and the list continues; treasures from the Father above, the creator of the universe and the giver of life.

How does one walk the high faith line? By believing, "For God so loved the world that He gave…." By confessing, "God have mercy on me a sinner." By receiving, "For by grace, you have been saved through faith and this is not your own doing it is the gift of God." By trusting, "Trust in the Lord with all your heart and lean not to your own understanding; in all your ways acknowledge   Him and He will make your paths straight." By listening, "Be still and know that I am God...."

By loving, "Love the Lord your God with all your heart and with all your soul and with all your strength and with all your mind and love your neighbor as yourself."

"Whatever is true, whatever is noble, whatever is right, whatever is pure...think about such things."

Dear Lord, thank you for treasures found at the high tide line on the beach and for treasures found on the high faith line in life. Jesus, thank you for love, mercy, grace, forgiveness, assurance, new beginnings and second chances. Thank you for the gift of abundance. Thank you for what is true, noble, and right. Empower us to think on such things. Thank you, Lord, for those who have led us in the past and for those who lead us today. In the name of Jesus Christ. Amen.

The Light

"I am the light of the world, he who follows me will not walk in darkness, but will have the light of life."
– John 8:12 (RSV)

Light! Among the many treasures that I have discovered by the sea is a man-made structure…a lighthouse. I am drawn to lighthouses. As a young boy, I remember climbing that first lighthouse, Point Loma, San Diego. Since then, I have made many climbs. I enjoy standing on the pier near the Village, in the evening, watching the beam of light penetrate the darkness.

Darkness! Two planes slammed into the towers and darkness gripped spouses, sons, daughters, loved ones, and families. A choice was made to misuse prescription medications and the darkness grew even darker. After thirty years of employment, termination came…a loss of employment, income, pension, health care and darkness flooded the soul. An angry word was spoken and darkness was present. The doctor walked into the hospital room filled with family and gave his report, "The cancer was inoperable" and darkness filled the room.

Can we find a place where we are told, we will not experience darkness? I think not. What we do find and hear is that we do not walk alone. By grace, we have been given "the light of life." Jesus spoke clearly…"Follow me."

Most of us have seen the beam of light from a lighthouse, penetrating the darkness. But it's limited. It's confined to space and time. It has a fixed location. The beam cannot be seen after twenty plus miles because of the curvature of the earth. The Lord's light is not limited! That's our experience! That's our affirmation! That's our testimony! His light is indeed the "light of the world." Wherever we find darkness, we find His light. "And the darkness has not overcome it!"

May we experience afresh daily the pure joy of His light flooding our souls!

"Father, we give you thanks for the light that is not confined by space or time. Lord, thank you for penetrating the darkness in our spirits and in our minds. Empower us to never deny the darkness, never to attempt to hide it. Give us grace and courage to walk through the darkness with you, day by day, hour by hour, moment by moment. In the name of the Father, of the Son, and of the Holy Spirit! Amen.

The Lighthouse – St. Simons Island – The beam from the light penetrated the darkness for that first time on September 1, 1872.

Week Three

"Then the Lord God said, 'It is not good
that man should be alone."
– Genesis 2:18 (NIV)

Channel Buoys

"One of those days Jesus went out to a mountainside to pray, and spent the night praying to God."
– Luke 6:12 (NIV)

It was another clear day on East Beach. It was beautiful. We were able to spot eight buoys. On most days, it's difficult to spot eight. These channel buoys mark the watery path for entrance through the sound and into safe harbor. Earliest written records of buoy markers go back to Spain in the thirteenth century. Buoys have improved over the centuries, but still provide basically the same function. Ultimately they aid in providing safe passage into harbor. When ships stay in the channel, they are protected from most of the hidden obstacles that often lay just below the surface.

What are some of the buoys that help keep us from hidden dangers in the channel we call life? What buoys open the way to joy, peace and love, for fulfillment and enrichment at home, in the work place, in interpersonal relationships, in financial concerns and in spiritual matters? What are they?

"Jesus went out to a mountainside to pray...." He spent the night in praying to God. His desire is that we, you and I, live in the channel of His grace and love. One of His buoys is prayer. Throughout His life and ministry, we see this buoy, this gift of prayer, keeping Him in the channel of His Father's grace and will; keeping Him safe from all those hidden obstacles that were alive and present in His day and still are in our day.

Some other buoys offering safe harbor are the study of the Word of God, the Bible, meditation, worship…both private and public, participating in the Lord's Supper, building meaningful spiritual relationships with brothers and sisters in Christ, finding a place of servanthood where joy, peace and love are fully experienced. The function of these buoys are to empower us to keep in the channel of His love and grace. Remember that hidden, but deadly obstacles are ever present. Remember His desire is to bless and to bring us into safe harbor!

Our Father, thank you the holy gift of prayer. Thank you for the gift of contact. Jesus, thank you for teaching us to pray. Lord, thank you for those buoys through the ages, who have saved many a weary sailor. Thank you, for the cross that reminds us of those unseen, but ever present deadly obstacles. Empower us to keep in the channel of your love and grace. In the name of Jesus Christ. Amen.

Casting Nets

"Put out into deep water, and let down the nets for a catch." Luke 5:4b "They were casting a net into the lake, for they were fishermen." – Matthew 4:18b (NIV)

Marvin Hood was an old salt and at home on the tidal creeks of the Savannah River Basin. He had lived on or near the water all of his life. An invitation from him to go out into the tidal creeks and cast nets for shrimp was better than any Super Bowl ticket, or even tickets for the Georgia/Florida football annual event.

It was late October, cool but pleasant, a cloudless sky. Actually, it was perfect. We were on the water early that morning. It was a first time adventure for this pastor. It didn't take very long to get the hang of casting the net. We were out for three hours. When we pulled up to his dock and weighed our catch, we had over one hundred pounds of shrimp. Yea!

Jesus' invitation to let down your nets is still very much alive. "And I will make you fishers of men."

We have been blessed by those who have said yes to His invitation and who have, through the years, cast nets of love, joy, peace and hope. I wouldn't be writing this and you would not be reading it without those who said yes. Marvin was one of those guys. My list is lengthy. I remember family, Sunday School Teachers, a Director of Youth, a caring friend, a brother in Christ, etc. Today, I still have those who cast nets of love for me. By God's grace, I continue to cast nets.

And in this day, in this hour, we are still invited to cast nets. There was great joy, when I came home with fifty pounds of shrimp. The Jensens and some neighbors ate well that night. Still, there is no greater joy than to cast nets in the name of our dear Lord and to see and experience the joy of a brother, or sister coming to understand love, joy, peace and hope in a fresh new light.

Dear Lord, thank you for those who have been obedient to your call to cast nets throughout the ages. Jesus, thank you for those who, with patience and kindness cast nets of love and joy in our lives. Lord, may we be known as men and women, who find deep joy in casting nets. Spirit of the living Lord, empower us to seek opportunities to cast nets. In the name of the Father, the Son, and the Holy Spirit. Amen.

Imagination

"Be devoted to one another in brotherly love. Honor one another above yourselves. Never be lacking in zeal, but keep your spiritual fervor, serving the Lord."
– Romans 12:10-11 (NIV)

He had that God-given gift called imagination. He was waiting for his dad and had some time alone. He put that time to great use. In the carport, there was a pole, about four to five feet long. A net was attached to one end. He looked to be about seven or eight. He picked up the pole and began with imagination and a good deal of enthusiasm.

First, the pole became a baton. He twirled and twisted it with great efficiency, using both hands. This went on for several minutes. Then, he became a drum major in the driveway, leading the band. Next, the pole became a rifle and he was defending his loved ones and his country from the enemy. The soldier in him took careful aim and was accurate with his shots. Celebrations would occur from time to time. Again, this went on for several minutes. Another transformation took place. The pole became a guitar. He strummed it with passion. Elvis had nothing on him. He had the moves and the voice, again several minutes passed. Finally, he shifted into a ninja. The pole was transformed once again into a lethal weapon. He was swift and accurate with each movement and thrust. At that moment, his dad came out of the house and they headed to the beach for a morning of fishing, but his imagination had been exercised with great pleasure.

She was a Down syndrome baby, but like this young boy, she had an imagination that was very alive. There was nothing timid about her God-given imagination. She understood being devoted, honoring one another, keeping the zeal, and serving the Lord. She had limits like all of us, but as with His imagination, she had her callings as well. Among many other ministries to honor one another and to serve God, she made it her spiritual practice to call each member of her church family, to wish them a Happy Birthday...and her church family was large, a thousand plus. She was open to His imagination, and open to what was next for her.

Thank you, dear Lord, for gifts of imagination. Dear Jesus, thank you for all those in our past, who used your God-given imagination to honor, to serve and to make that critical difference for each of us. Empower us to be open to your God-given gift of imagination, to your spirit. In His holy name. Amen.

Just Do It

"The wind blows where it wills…." John 3:8 (RSV)
"But they who wait on the Lord shall renew their strength, they shall mount up with wings like eagles, they shall run and not be weary, they shall walk and not faint."
– Isaiah 40:31 (RSV)

Seagulls do it! Terns do it. Pelicans and sandpipers do it. Even snakebirds do it. What is it they do?

There was a stiff wind coming out of the northeast. They were facing that head wind in unison. They were designed to face the wind. If they moved to the left or to the right, they easily lose their balance. Check it out. You will even find them in the rest position facing the wind. They also like to flock together. There is strength in numbers.

Facing that wind, also gives them a quick start. The wind lifts them up and even offers protection from those who would be considered a threat. I have watched dogs come just a little too close. It's a beautiful thing to see them take flight together.

Just do it! Brothers and sisters in Christ do it! Do what? They face toward the wind of the Spirit together. They allow the wind of the Holy Spirit to lift them up. While resting or laboring, they are always in the ready position, ready for flight and for service. Again, please check it out!

They also flock together. Brothers and sisters in Christ offer care to one another. They reach out beyond their comfort zones to others. They are open to His call. They flock together for support, encouragement, accountability, and challenge. Prayer, worship, study, service are high priorities. They "make a joyful noise." They find joy in celebration. They honor Jesus Christ daily. Most importantly, they "wait on the Lord...."

Father, thank you for wind and for the wind of the Holy Spirit. Thank you for giving us very clear directions. Lord God, forgive us when we fail to make preparations, or to be ready. Lord, give us grace to just do it. Empower us to wait in expectation on the Spirit of the living God. Move us beyond our comfort zones. In the name of the one who taught and still teaches us to be prepared. Amen.

Facing the easterly wind together on East Beach.

A Christmas Nest

"Even the sparrow has found a home, and the swallow a nest for herself, where she may have her young --- a place near your altar, O Lord Almighty, my King and my God."
– Psalm 84:3 (NIV)

Nests are essential. Without them, life is severely damaged, even tragically lost.

It was a couple of weeks before Christmas. The cold, nasty, and windy weather had arrived. Leaves were falling earlier than normal from the small native scrubs, weeds and trees that line the marsh by Ocean Road. In the spring, a nest had been carefully designed and placed, so that it was unseen and protected. And so it was. The leaves were gone now and it was easily seen and totally unprotected, a Christmas nest sighting for sure. The occupants of the nest had long moved on. Be assured of this, for a season, caring and nurturing took place in that nest. Both were essential and necessary for life.

It was another age, another time and another place, still caring and nurturing occurred. It was a place where God's creatures gave birth to their offspring: sparrows, swallows, cows, donkeys, sheep, etc. Each experienced vital nurture and tender care. This is God's Holy Design.

In that lowly birthing, (nesting), place, "a child was born, and a Son was given." He was helpless and received what was essential for His life: love, care, nurture, and peace. Again, it was God's Holy Design! This child and His parents ultimately moved on with love and with grace and the world was changed forever.

His day and our day have striking similarities. The idea of God's Holy Design was in question in His day and still is in our day. The reality of God was in question as well and so it is today. Forgetting, denying and rejecting God and His Holy Design occurred then and still does, although, it is so very sad, tragic and heartbreaking when it does.

Almighty God, we give thanks to you for those who provided a birthing place, a place of nurture and care for "a child, a Son." Lord Jesus, we give thanks for the nurture and care that we have received in our yesterdays and that we will receive in our tomorrows. Lord, forgive us when we forget, when we deny, when we reject. Empower us to be open to the possibilities around us to offer nurture and care. Keep our hearts, minds, souls and spirits focused. In His name. Amen.

Bloody Marsh, Ocean Road and 14th Street, East Beach.

The Treasure Hunter

"But we have this treasure in jars of clay to show that this all-surpassing power comes from God and not from us."
– II Corinthians 4:7 (NIV)

Gently, he waved his arm back and forth. He was in search of treasure. The wand moved to and fro just above the sand. His earphones were in place. He listened intently. He was listening for just that right sound. This treasure hunter was in no hurry. He moved slowly across the beach. He seemed to be out of place on this hot July day. He looked more like a farmer than a treasure hunter, with his wide brim hat and long sleeves and long pants.

Clearly he was a veteran. He had been here before. He had been successful many times. He had found engagement rings, class rings, wedding bands, ear rings, bracelets, watches, necklaces, etc.

"WE HAVE THIS TREASURE."

How? "This all surpassing power comes from God and not from us." It doesn't come from us. This treasure comes from the one who seeks us out one by one, moment by moment, Jesus Christ. It comes from the Spirit of the Living Lord that never gives up, the Holy Spirit. Never!

What is this treasure in jars of clay, in earthen vessels? The Church! The Body of Christ! It is those who say "YES" and live that "YES" out day by day. Do we see this treasure in jars of clay? What a difference this treasure makes in my life, in your life and in the lives of countless others.

My treasure hunter friend says, "My greatest joy comes when I am able to return a lost treasure to its rightful owner." The greatest joy in heaven comes when one who was lost is found...when ultimately one says, "Yes!"

Father God, thank you for this treasure in earthen vessels. Thank you for the Body of Christ, the Church. Thank you, dear Jesus, for those in the Body, who have helped to make the difference, not only in our lives, but also in the lives of many others. Thank you for their faithful obedience. Father, empower in each of us that same obedience. In the name of the one who still provides this treasure in jars of clay. Amen.

For the Loners

"Then the Lord God said, 'It is not good that man should be alone." – Genesis 2:18 (NIV)

One October morning, on the beach I said, "Lord, I'm listening." They were headed south. The ducks were in their famous "V" shaped formation. It was a beautiful sighting.

Ducks do better together. They do better when the load is shared. The leader of the formation changes from time to time, because he or she faces the greatest wind resistance; to be in front of the "V" constantly is tiring. The "V" formation is not on the same level, it's tiered! The duck, in flapping his or her wings, creates an upward lift for the duck that follows. Working together in a team effort, they are able to travel greater distances. Specialists in aerodynamics affirm that the whole flock has a 71% greater flying range, than if each bird flies alone. That's truly amazing!

Alone! There are those among us who are tempted to fly alone. Somewhere along the way, the testimony that says, "I don't need anyone. I can take care of myself and don't need any help," becomes a reality. I understand those feelings. By the time I was seventeen, we had moved over twenty times. My father was in the Navy. My grandfather was a Methodist minister. I learned early to be a loner and that I didn't need anyone, but God. But by the grace of God, I learned that's not the truth. It's a lie. At times, I still struggle with the loner in me, but in those times, I am reminded by love that I need others.

Jesus needed others. He knew we would, too. He first called His disciples and then He called others to follow. Then He called us. Jesus Christ gave us the Body. We call that Body the church. Paul calls it "the Body of Christ!" It is not "I am the church." It is "We are the church together!"

Ducks do better together and so do we.

Lord, thank you for designing us to be in relationship. Thank you for making us in your own image. Protect us from the loner temptation. Empower us to recognize the truth that we are not alone. Help us to receive support and to offer support day by day. In the name of the one who calls us together. Amen.

Week Four

"Therefore I tell you, do not be anxious about your life…"
"Look at the birds of the air: they neither sow nor reap nor
gather into barns, and yet your heavenly Father feeds them.
Are you not of more value than they?"
– Matthew 6:25a, 26 (RSV)

Rejoicing

"This is the day the Lord has made; let us rejoice and be glad in it." – Psalm 118:24 (NIV)

Her name was Happy. My wife gave her that name, because it seemed to us that she was the happiest dog we had ever seen on the beach. Her tail never stopped wagging. We thought that if Happy was not careful, one day her tail might just simply fall off from overuse. She loved the beach. I think her greatest joy was wading in little ponds looking for small fish and shrimp. She was always a refreshing sight.

Most dogs enjoy the beach. They like the wide open space. They celebrate the freedom to romp and play. Some enjoy jumping into the water and swimming. Others relish the opportunity of running and chasing birds. Still others love fetching balls hurled by their masters. And then there are those who are masters at catching Frisbees.

Lord, what word do you have for us from our four legged friends; from Happy? "Rejoice in the day...Celebrate the moment...Carpe Diem...Seize the day... Allow time for that little child in you to come out...play and rejoice!"

Remember Jesus' experience with Mary and Martha. Mary sat at the Lord's feet, and listened. Martha on the other hand was distracted with serving...an important thing. Martha asked Jesus to tell Mary to get up and help out with the serving. Jesus answered Martha with these loving and challenging words, "Martha, Martha, you are anxious and troubled about many things; one thing is needful. Mary has chosen the good portion, which shall not be taken from her." There is a choice to be made every day, every moment!

Our four legged friends, especially the one named Happy, invites us to "Rejoice in the day". We are encouraged by the spirit of the living Lord to "Rejoice in the Lord always!"

Lord God, we thank you for placing in the human spirit that need for rejoicing and celebrating. Thank you for Jesus, the one who took rejoicing and celebrating to the highest level. In the name of the one who stills says with love, "Mary has chosen the good portion." Amen.

Happy, East Beach Resident.

Rejoicing in the moment.

Overloaded

"Cast all your anxiety on Him because he cares about you."
– I Peter 5:7 (NIV)

The container vessel slowly made its way up the channel. We watched as it floated by. It was huge. We were having lunch on Savannah's water front. I noticed the mark about mid-ship, just above the water line; a circle, a vertical line and several horizontal lines dissecting the vertical line. I had often wondered what it meant. I asked my friend if he knew. His response was, "Yes. That's the 'Plimsoll Mark.' It is a load-line marking."

A ship loaded to the "Plimsoll Mark" is carrying the maximum cargo for her design. If the water line goes above that mark the ship is in danger of sinking. In the 1800s and earlier, many ships and sailors were lost at sea, because ship owners often overloaded their ships. They were seeking larger profits. Bigger loads produced greater returns. Samuel Plimsoll was a member of the British Parliament and a merchant himself. He fought for a law stopping this immoral practice. He became known as "the sailor's friend." The law was passed. The name of the law was the Merchant Shipping Act of 1876.

Have you ever felt overloaded? The doctor said to me, "You are going to have by-pass surgery!" After seven heart by-passes, a pacemaker and four stints, I have on occasion felt overloaded. I experienced those emotions that human beings have, when they suffer loss. I have my own set of whys. I have at times struggled with denial, anxiety, doubt, fear, anger, guilt, depression, etc.

I am reminded that I am very human. We can overload our lives; our ships very easily. You would think we would learn. I am also reminded again and again that we have one who understands that reality. One who offers an alternative, a "Plimsoll Mark," if you please. "Be still and know that I am God." "Trust in God with all your heart." "Lean not to your own understanding." "Cast all your anxiety on Him, because He cares for you."

Lord God, we thank you. We thank you for understanding how easy it is for us to become overloaded. Often we fail to recognize our limits. Empower us to carry our share of the load with passion and grace. Teach us where the "Plimsoll Mark" is on this pilgrimage. In the name of the one who calls on His children to trust Him. Amen

The Plimsoll, a load bearing mark.

For a man who fought the good fight.

Jumping Waves

"After this, the word of the Lord came to Abram in a vision: 'Do not be afraid, Abram, I am your shield, your very great reward." – Genesis 15:1 (NIV)

It was one of those teachable moments. Father and daughter were in ankle deep water…his ankles. He was showing her how to jump the waves. She was probably less than two and consequently the water was a little deeper for her. A wave would break and he would jump. She watched him carefully. He made several jumps and finally she moved back toward the water's edge. When a smaller wave came, she jumped herself.

She clearly exercised "the small step approach". Where her dad had jumped the water was just a little too deep for her. The fear factor was higher there. Moving back to the water's edge, the fear factor wasn't quite as large. She jumped the waves, again and again. The more she jumped, the more her confidence grew.

"The small step approach" works. It worked for Abraham. The water was too deep and he acknowledged his doubt. It worked for Moses. Again, the water was too deep. It worked for King David…too deep. It worked for the disciples. They all ultimately began where they could. "Take that first step, (that first jump), and I, the Lord, will be with you." And their confidence grew and grew!

Health issues and financial concerns have and can put us in water that is too deep. Broken relationships have and can put us there too; spiritual questionings have and can as well. The fear factor clearly comes into play.

"The small step approach" still works. The little jumper reminds us to exercise it, in relationship, to that health issue, to that financial concern, to that broken relationship, and to that spiritual questioning. What step needs to be taken now?

Abraham, Moses, David and the disciples, all took that "first small step."

Lord God, thank you for a little girl who took a small step on a big beach. Thank you for a father who encouraged her with love and for his being present with her. Thank you, Jesus, for encouraging us to take those small steps and for your promise to always be with us. Empower us to encourage others to take that small step. In the name of the one who is called Emmanuel. Amen.

Direction

"Thy word is a lamp to my feet, and a light to my path."
– Psalm 119:105 (RSV)

I enjoy the beach in the mornings most of all. The mornings
I walk on the beach before the sunrise, I find great joy in
locating the North Star. It's easy to find. First, find the big
dipper. The big dipper makes a circuit around the North
Star. The outer edge of the big dipper, opposite the handle
edge, always points towards the North Star. The North
Star has given direction to many a seafarer and still does
today, even with all of our technology.

I need direction, more than just north or south, east or
west. I have often gone in directions that were not beneficial
to my well-being, or to the well-being of anyone else.
Remember the old saying, "I was in the wrong place, at the
wrong time, with the wrong people." I have been there and
I have done that. Again, I stand in need of direction.

After my grandmother's death, my mother gave me her
Bible. It has been, indeed, a priceless treasure. Her Bible
was her North Star. She found direction for living her life
through that book. At the close of her day, she knelt in
prayer, crawled into bed, and read from the Word of God
until sleep came. I watched it happen many times. She had
direction. Each Sunday, she joined others in turning to
the book. When the sun was shining at its brightest, she
turned to the book. When the day was darkest, filled with
uncertainty, she turned to the book.

God used her actions to point one of His children, her grandson, in a much needed direction. One day, that grandson picked up the book himself and slowly, but surely found a new direction for his life. He found a direction that offered a new way of living, a life filled with love, joy, hope and peace.

Still he struggles and he is far from perfect, far from where he desires to be, but he is on the path and he does receive blessed direction.

Father, thank you for your loving direction. Thank you for the North Star. Thank you for the Bible. Lord, thank you for a "light upon our paths." Father, thank you for Jesus Christ, "the light of the world." Lord, lead us on a plain path. Teach us to love. In the name of Jesus Christ. Amen.

Distinguishing Marks

"Therefore I tell you, do not be anxious about your life…"
"Look at the birds of the air; they neither sow, nor reap,
nor gather into barns, and yet your heavenly Father feeds
them. Are you not of more value than they?"
– Matthew 6:25a, 26 (RSV)

The seagull hopped along on one leg, his only distinguishing
mark from all the others. Somewhere on his journey he had
lost a leg. It was clear his loss had not stopped him. He
moved about as well as any of his friends. And when he
took flight, he was equal to his brothers and to his sisters.
Our God cares for His creation, "even the birds of the air."

Like my friend, the one-legged seagull, J.D. had his own
distinguishing mark. J.D. lost both feet. He had just
retired. He was diabetic. On his first home visit from the
V.A. Hospital, a mutual friend came by to help him get out
of bed and into a wheel chair. As J.D. pushed himself into
the living room, he turned and said, "Herbert, hand me my
slippers!" There was a moment of silence. Then everyone
broke out into laughter. J.D. was beginning to take flight
without feet. His loss did not stop him.

J.D. lost his feet and was in danger of losing much more.
I remember those early visits to the hospital. He had a
simple plea, "Jim, give me something to kill myself." He
had lost his will to live. He desired death. J.D. experienced
those natural emotions that come with loss, especially great
loss. My friend struggled mightily with anger, depression,
denial, resentment, bitterness, guilt, etc. He was angry with

God, "Why God?" He was angry with others, "Why can't you do something?" He was angry with himself, "Why was I not more sensitive to the needs of my body?"

I asked J.D. one day, "How are you making it?" His voice was clear and strong, "Only by the grace of God, our Father, and by the support of the brothers and sisters God gives me!"

Father, thank you for not giving up on us. Thank you for those words, "are you not of more value…" Thank you for the gift of life and the gift of flight. Lord, help us always remember that you never give up. In the name of Jesus Christ, our friend and our Savior. Amen.

Be of good courage! Never give up!

Fight the good fight! Keep the faith!

A Tug of War

"No one can serve two masters." – Matthew 6:24 (NIV)

It was an early morning hour. The beach is dog friendly. Dogs and their masters were out in force. They are like a small community: groupings of families. Sunday mornings seem to be the best dog times. In that early hour, most vacationers and beachcombers were still sleeping. It was a sight to behold.

On this particular day, a new sighting occurred. Two large dogs had a rope, five to six feet long. One had one end of the rope, the other dog had the other end. They were in a royal tug of war. One pulled, the other pulled back. I watched for a good while. When I finally walked away, they were still going at it.

After a time of reflection, *Star Wars* came to mind. This science fiction epic is filled with tugs of war that take place daily even hourly; faith or fear, freedom or slavery, peace or war, light or darkness, right or wrong, good or evil. Luke and Darth Vader experienced tugs of war. The list grows. Stay in bed and deny or get up and acknowledge. Take a stand, or walk away. Tugs of war are personal, relational, communal, and spiritual. To deny them is unhealthy and possibly deadly spiritually, emotionally and physically.

Listen with love to our heavenly Father's responses to tugs of war; between fear and faith, slavery and freedom, "I have come to set the prisoner free"…war and peace, "Peace I leave with you; my peace I give you…Do not let your hearts be troubled, and do not be afraid…" light and darkness, "I am the light of the world. Whoever follows me, will never walk in darkness, but will have the light of life"…right and wrong, "He leads me in paths of right living…." and good and evil, "Let us not lose heart in doing good.", "Deliver us from evil."

Again, listen with love to His Spirit within. "Choose for yourselves this day, whom you will serve…. But as for me and my family we will serve the Lord." "No one can serve two masters."

Dear Father, thank you for understanding the tugs of war from within and from without. Jesus, thank you for new mercies and for a fresh new day. Lord, deliver us from living out cheap grace. Empower us to choose grace with great compassion, commitment and zeal. In His holy name. Amen.

Normandy Beach

"And he took bread, gave thanks and broke it, and gave it to them, saying, "This is my body given for you; do this in remembrance of me." – Luke 22:19 (NIV)

The tide was high. There was wonderful cloud cover, humidity was low, and the wind was steadily coming out of the south. It was another perfect time to be on the beach on a July day. It was great for listening within. She appeared right at the moment my thoughts turned inward. She was enjoying the beach with a friend like so many others. Her tee-shirt got my full attention, inscribed on her shirt in bold black letters were Normandy Beach. The sounds of surf were soothing and calming. The beach, the surf, listening within and the Normandy Beach tee-shirt took me down a spiritual remembrance path.

Normandy Beach, the year was 1944. June 2014 on the sixth, freedom loving people across the world remembered once again. It was the 70th remembrance. In 1944, 156,115 allied troops invaded Europe, many landed on Normandy Beach, to bring freedom and justice to a people enslaved and without justice. Many did not survive that day. Freedom and justice have always been costly and will always be so. My dad was in England on that day, U.S. Navy. He helped prepare airplanes for that hour. He remembered being awakened by the rumble of the planes flying overhead on their way to Normandy and beyond.

In the year of our Lord, 2017, around the world, across Georgia, in Atlanta, in the Golden Isles, freedom loving people and justice seekers still gather together to remember on the Lord's Day. We remember freedom and justice are very costly. We remember we stand on the shoulders of those who have come before and have paid that ultimate price. We remember that ultimate freedom and justice comes through Jesus Christ and Him alone. "This is my body given for you, do this in remembrance of me." "He has sent me to proclaim freedom…to release the oppressed…" Paul writes, "Where the Spirit of the Lord is, there is freedom."

We remember!

Author of liberty, freedom and justice, we give you thanks. We give you thanks for "the Spirit that testifies with our spirits, that we are children of God." That indeed, we are free by your grace and mercy. Empower us to be fruitful and faithful servants of this divine freedom and justice. In His holy name. Amen.

Week Five

"Nathanael said to him, 'Can anything good come out of
Nazareth?' Philip said to him, 'Come and see.'"
– John 1:46

"Come, see a man who told me all that I ever did.
Can this be the Christ?"
– John 4:29(RSV)

"Whiter than Snow"

"Cleanse me with hyssop, and I will be clean; wash me, and I will be whiter than snow." – Psalm 51:7 (NIV)

We live on one of the Golden Isles of Georgia, Saint Simons Island, in the midst of the "Marshes of Glynn". From time to time, the marsh purges itself of the old and prepares for the new. In those times, we find remnants of the old scattered up and down the beach. It makes a real mess and on rare occasion, smells to high heaven; not a pleasant odor.

When we have high tides and the water currents are just right, the beach can be (whisked) swept clean in one motion. The remnants of the old are taken out to sea, or scattered in another location along the coast. All that is left afterwards is a clean, fresh beach.

I have a friend who is a retired minister, who just recently celebrated his one hundredth birthday. Leonard and I were sharing thoughts about ministry. Both of us had found ministry to be filled with great joy. I asked him, "What was the best part of ministry for you?"

He shared this experience. There was a lady in the congregation, who was very faithful and deeply committed. She could be counted on when called upon. She was a willing servant. One day, she came to see him and shared a heart concern. She said, "You know me and know my willingness to serve." She went on, "Something's wrong. After all these years of servicing, I am feeling an emptiness.

Something seems to be missing. Do you have any suggestions or thoughts?"

He turned and picked up a blank three by five card and offered it to her. He then said, "What did you just do?" "I took the card." "Again what did you just do?" "I accepted it." Leonard said, "That's what needs to happen. We need to accept His grace afresh daily, often moment by moment." Whenever we fully accept, we are completely "washed whiter than snow!"

Dear Father, thank you for your desire to wash us "whiter than snow." Thank you, Lord Jesus, for taking up the cross and washing us "whiter than snow." Empower us to be open to your grace and your cleansing power, day by day, moment by moment. Help us to share your desire. In His holy name. Amen.

Beyond the Horizon

"For to me, to live is Christ and to die is gain."
– Philippians 1:21 (NIV)

Among the many treasures found by the sea is the horizon. It's easily missed. Maybe it's missed, because it is ever present. We human beings tend to miss things that are constantly before us. The horizon is the place where sky and sea seem to touch, but there is more. Beyond every horizon, there is a physical beyond, an emotional beyond, and a spiritual beyond.

A young teen with his mom and his younger brother spent twenty-eight days aboard a ship on the open sea headed toward that ever moving horizon and a happy reunion with his dad. The teen had a practice of observing the 360 degree horizon that was ever present. Often, he looked forward, past the bow of the USS Morton, a military transport, toward the future beyond the horizon. He saw adventure, challenge and opportunity. He saw home, family, love, peace and acceptance. Also, he felt anxious, fearful, troubled, and doubtful; all natural feelings for human beings experiencing change and loss, especially a young teen. Occasionally in those doubt filled times, he looked back toward the stern and focused on the past but ultimately returned to the bow toward the future.

On the twenty-eighth day, the teen's family was reunited on the docks of the Port of Manila, Philippines. It was a physical and an emotional reunion, but more so it was a spiritual one. It was truly beyond the horizon. I was that teen and still remember. We had disembarked from San Francisco, California in June 1954.

Saint Paul was in prison in Rome. It was dark and the hour was clearly uncertain. There were no horizons to be seen. Paul had seen the horizon on the beach, on the open sea and had claimed the beyond. In this hour of darkness, Paul writes with love, hope, compassion and assurance, "For to me to live is Christ and to die is gain." He was prepared to live abundantly..."to live is Christ." He was also prepared to die..."to die is gain." He was prepared for home..."A house not made with hands, eternal..."a home filled with family, love, and peace.

Father, creator of the universe and planet Earth, we give thanks to you for the tender treasure of life abundant, for the precious gift of each new horizon, and for the Holy reality of "a house not made with hands," a home eternal. Jesus, open doors for us to share what we have so freely received. In your holy name. Amen.

"Come and See"

"Nathanael said to him, 'Can anything good come out of Nazareth?' Philip said to him, 'Come and see.'"
– John 1:46.
"Come, see a man who told me all that I ever did. Can this be the Christ?" – John 4:29 (RSV)

I watched the fisherman pull in his catch. It was a shell. He was on the rocks, fishing next to Gould's inlet. I told him, "It's a mighty fine shell." His young son called out to his older sister, "Come and see, the shell that daddy caught!" Because of the wind and the distance, she didn't hear him and didn't respond. When I got closer to his sister, she was calling out to him, "Come and see. I've got a crab!" He didn't hear her and didn't respond.

Those words "Come and see" continued to echo in my spirit and in my soul.

How many times have I heard, "come and see" and not responded? There were those who were saying to me with love, "Come and see." I was too far away to hear. The reality was in my private little world, I had my own "come and see." I was not ready to see, or to hear.

I remember a young man when I was far away. His name was Jimmy Harris. He was from Pitts, Georgia. "Come and see!" I don't know if he ever said those exact words, but by his action, by his walk, he encouraged that genuine need in my spirit. There have been many others, who by loving action continued to encourage that need in my soul.

Can you identify with me? Do you have a name, someone who encouraged that need in you?

There came a moment in time in my own life, when I felt I had to share by my actions and also by my words, "Come and see." At that moment, life changed for me.

Father, thank you for the Spirit that testifies with our spirits that indeed we do belong to you. Lord God, thank you for the Spirit that says "come and see." Thank you for those in our past, in our present, and in our future who have encouraged, who do encourage and who will encourage. Help us to be encouragers as well. In the name of Jesus Christ. Amen.

Protect or Pollute

"With the tongue we praise our Lord and Father, and with it we curse men, who have been made in God's likeness."
– James 3:9 (NIV)

It was an October morning, a "Chamber of Commerce" day, on the beach! The temperature was in the seventies. The humidity was low. There was a gentle breeze coming out of the north. It felt wonderful! The sky was blue with a few cumulus clouds moving lazily above land and sea. The tide was low. The beach was pristine, clean and beautiful. It was a treasure, another gift from the Father of all creation.

The temperature, the humidity, the gentle breeze, the sky, the clouds, and the tide were magnificent. It happens more often than not. But on this day, the beach was not pristine. This God given treasure had been polluted by litter and trash. There had been a huge party. There were those present at that party, who only thought of self and their own pleasure. The beach had again been polluted. We have seen it before and will see it again.

With judgmental thoughts rolling around in my head, I was reminded of these words. "With the tongue we praise our Lord and Father and with it we curse men!" With the tongue we protect and with it we pollute! Some of us understand how easy it is to pollute with word and thought. Most of us have had to deal with that particular battle. We would never pollute the creation we have been given. We have, by His holy grace and by His tender spirit, moved passed that. Still we have polluted the air with words that were harmful and should not have been spoken. These words from James came to mind as well..."Be quick to listen, slow to speak and slow to anger."

Each new day, we are given a choice. We can praise or curse. We can protect or pollute. We make the choice! His invitation is clear. He invites us to praise and to protect. His promise is to bless our efforts.

Father God, thank you for the beauty of your creation. Thank you for the precious gift of life on this small planet. Jesus, thank you for grace and mercy. Be merciful unto us. We stand in need of your mercy. Forgive us when we pollute. Empower us to know the difference between the two; pollution and protection. In the name of the Father, Son, and Holy Spirit. Amen.

Join the Team.

New Signs

"This will be a sign to you: You will find a baby wrapped in cloths and lying in a manger." – Luke 2:12 (NIV)

DANGER
WATER COVERS SANDBAR
10' DEPTH AT HIGH TIDE
STRONG CURRENTS

We have been given new signs on our beach. At times, we have had some very vicious rip tides. Through the years, there have been those who have lost their lives because they ignore the posted warnings. Others have been caught unaware of the hidden, but very real danger. Still, lives have been lost. The water can look so inviting and so refreshing, peaceful even. The new signs have been placed on sandbars for the purpose of hopefully and prayerfully saving lives.

"I was sinking deep in sin, far from the peaceful shore. Very deeply stained with-in, sinking to rise no more. But the Master of the sea heard my despairing cry, from the waters lifted me-Now safe am I. Love lifted me...." James Rowe and Howard Smith in Saugatuck, Connecticut, in 1912, created this musical offering...James with words and Howard with notes.

They echo the experience of others, who came before; like Paul, Peter, James and John. The Wesley brothers affirm that same spiritual encounter. There are those who have confirmed those "sinking deep in sin and love lifted me moments" in life. Life is filled with dangerous rip currents.

Drowning still occurs. Many of us have been blessed to have family and dear friends, who have affirmed for us the danger, the love and the choice. The writer of Hebrews puts it clearly…"Therefore, since we are surrounded by such a great cloud of witnesses, let us run with perseverance the race marked out for us."

"For the Son of man came to seek and to save the lost." "This will be a sign to you: You will find a baby…." We have a sign!

Thank you, dear Father, for the sign. Dear Lord, thank you for the baby who became a man. Thank you Jesus, for lifting love and sustaining grace. Forgive us when we fail to remember, we have been saved by your tender touch. Empower us to be signs in this day and in this hour. In His holy name. Amen.

Sandcastle Building 101

"The crowds that went before him and those that followed shouted, 'Hosanna to the Son of David!', 'Blessed is he who comes in the name of the Lord!', 'Hosanna in the highest!'" – Matthew 21:9 (RSV)

There were six children on the beach, beginning to build sandcastles with a bucket. Turrets were already shaped into their bucket. The children ranged in age from probably five to ten. The ten-year-old young lady seemed to be in charge. They filled the bucket. She carefully patted it down. She turned it over and began gently tapping the sides. One of the younger ones was given the opportunity of lifting the bucket. It was perfect! It didn't crumble, crack or fall apart! With one voice they broke out cheering, "Yeah! Yeah! YEAH!" They celebrated their success with sandcastle building. It was a triumphant moment. The victorious and uplifting sound was treasured by this observer. In a span of about ten minutes, there were five more castles.

There is within the human spirit that need for "Yeah!" moments. Without them, life becomes very barren, even deadly. We need them and are designed for them! We can see "Yeah!" moments all around us, when we look carefully. They come in a thousand different ways; making sandcastles with friends, getting that first hit at the plate, balancing on a bike for the first time, cooking that first batch of brownies, passing the exam for a driver's license, graduating from High School, receiving that first pay check, standing at the altar with your beloved, holding in your arms a new born, gathering with others on the Lord's Day to say thank you once again, and the list goes on and on.

"Hosanna to the Son of David!" "Hosanna in the highest!" The crowds on that day, so long ago could not hold it in. They had seen and they had heard. It was indeed a "Yeah" moment in the human spirit. It was a triumphant celebration. Little did they know, how great a moment it would ultimately become. They did not understand the events of the week ahead, or comprehend what they would mean. Christ carefully laid the foundation and was preparing to hand the building of His Kingdom on earth to His followers. And so He did! And so He does!

Lord Jesus, thank you for sandcastle building and for kingdom building on earth. Thank you for those "Yeah!" moments in life. Lord, give us grace and wisdom to be Kingdom Builders in this day and in this hour. In His holy name. Amen.

Taps at Twilight

"And he took bread, gave thanks and broke it, and gave it to them, saying, 'This is my body given for you: do this in remembrance of me.'" – Luke 22:19 (NIV)

Over a thousand gathered, young and old alike. It was another Memorial Day remembrance, truly an awesome treasure by the sea. We gathered to remember and honor those who sacrificed the ultimate, so that we might live in freedom.

The band played patriotic music. The sun was slowly making its descent in the west. There was an impromptu fly by, a bright blue and yellow trainer, a throwback to the early forties, added to the excitement of the moment. The pilot made two passes. Then another impromptu event occurred. We heard the horn blow three times and knew a ship was moving out toward the open sea. This mammoth structure slipped slowly through the sound. In a few minutes, we heard another horn, again three blasts. They were passing side by side, another large ship was inward bound. Also, while these events occurred, three commercial jets, high in the sky, were highlighted by the setting sun. Beautiful!

This all happened before General Mundy, the thirtieth Commandant of the United States Marines Corps, stood to speak. The stage was set and he was not found wanting. He was outstanding. He recognized the citizen soldier, as compared to the professional one. He encouraged with gentleness, the young ones present to always remember and never forget. Taps was played. We remembered all those who have sacrificed the ultimate, and all those who serve today.

And Jesus took bread, gave thanks and broke it. "Do this in remembrance...." We do remember! For over two thousand years, there are those who have remembered. There is a long line, who have said, "Yes!" He paid the ultimate price for freedom from all that would enslave us. There are those who have followed and also paid an ultimate price. This hour, Christ holds us in the palm of His hand. We stand on the shoulders of our Savior and of those saints who have gone before. Young ones, remember!

Father God, we thank you for those who loved you and country more than self. Jesus, thank you for the holy sacramental gift of freedom. May we be numbered in that body that remembers daily, often even hourly, that you paid the ultimate price and that others have joined in paying that price as well. In His holy name. Amen.

I pledge allegiance to the flag of the United States of America, and to the Republic for which it stands: one nation under God....

Week Six

"For we know that if the earthly tent we live in is destroyed, we have a building from God, a house not made with hands, eternal in the heavens."

– II Corinthians 5:1 (RSV)

Fear and Hope

"I have set my rainbow in the clouds, and it will be a sign of the covenant between me and the earth." "Whenever the rainbow appears in the clouds, I will see it and remember the everlasting covenant...." – Genesis 9:13,16a (NIV)

It was the first day of autumn in an early morning hour. It was cool and there was a soft rain. The wind was coming from the east; from the ocean. The rain felt refreshing. It lasted for only a few minutes. I made my way to the water's edge and looked toward the sun. It was hidden by a cluster of clouds. The blue sky was filled with clouds. Some were gray and seemed to be laden with water. Others were bright white and fluffy. From around the perimeter of clouds, streaks of light shot out and filled the horizon. I had no eagerness to move past the beauty and majesty of that moment. He truly refreshed my soul.

I turned to leave and there it was; a rainbow. The colors were vivid and alive. I stood in awe. I turned once more to see the streaks of light and turned again to leave and saw a double rainbow. Stopping in my tracks, the message was clear for me. HOPE! Remember!

We live in a day filled with darkness and despair. Fear and doubt rule in many quarters. Hopelessness is alive and well. I thought of God and the light he offers day by day. "The light shines in the darkness and the darkness has not overcome it!" I thought of brothers and sisters in our world, in our land, in our communities, in our churches, and in our families who are walking in days and nights filled with clouds, darkness and fear. Everywhere we turn we see them. They have names and faces. I know some of them by name. One in seven today are unemployed, not lazy...unemployed! That does not include all those who are under employed, or all those who struggle, too often silently.

Dear Father, give us strength and wisdom to give our very best, to not falter, and to wait with hope. Dear Jesus, thank you for giving your very best, for waiting with hope and never giving up on us. Thank you, again for the light that shines in our darkness and for the rainbow that still offers hope. Thank you for the precious gift of hope. Help us, dear Lord, to be light bearers in the midst of fear, despair, and doubt. Empower us to commit and to shine brightly, to penetrate the fear and the doubt with compassion, love and hope. In the name of the one who proclaimed, "I am the light of the world...." Amen.

The Kite Man

"But you will receive power when the Holy Spirit has come upon you; and you will be my witnesses in Jerusalem, and in all Judea and Samaria, and to the ends of the earth."
– Acts 1:8 (RSV)

Power! Do you like kites? I do. The Kite Man was on the beach again. This fellow from England always adds beauty and excitement for a regular beachcomber like myself. His kites are not your typical kites. They are huge and fill the sky with colors of the rainbow; bright reds, yellows, blues and greens. They come in all shapes and sizes. There is even a bigger than life "Garfield." I would guess some are eight by ten feet with tails extending fifty feet or more. In the past, I have counted five kites being lifted by powerful winds along the coast.

The Englishman understands the necessity of waiting for power. He waits patiently and eagerly for that power. Power that will lift his kites upward toward heaven. When the time is right, he's on the beach. He tenderly places his kites in position to be lifted up by the power of the winds. For the little boy still alive in me, it is a magnificent sight.

Simon Peter, Andrew, James, and John, who were the first to say "yes" to the Lord's invitation, learned about waiting for power, for the precious wind of God, the Holy Spirit. "But you will receive power...." They experienced the universal and timeless emotions that are commonly associated with grief; shock, denial, pain, sadness, fear, doubt, questionings, anger, guilt, depression, brokenness, and acceptance. They waited to receive. They waited in faithful obedience.

Those who wait in faithful obedience are lifted up and become witnesses of the living Lord. Everything changes within. Obstacles still come and go; grief will be known again, but that power that lifts up will remain forever.

Recall those who have waited in your life, who have received power from above and who have witnessed with love and compassion.

Dear Lord, thank you for your call to wait. Empower us to be faithfully obedient, until we have received power. By your divine grace, may we be numbered among those who bring beauty and excitement to life. May we be your witnesses "to the ends of the earth." In the name of the Holy Spirit! Amen.

The power of the winds on the earth lifts above.

Waiting with patience and love for power from on high.

Constant

"For the Lord is good; his steadfast love endures forever, and his faithfulness to all generations."
– Psalm 100:5 (RSV)

Living by the sea, one quickly learns about the tide. We walk the beach almost daily and the tide always determines where we walk. A high tide keeps us off the beach. No matter what happens in the world, during any twenty-four hour period, the tide comes in and goes out twice. It is constant!

Years ago, our family and one of our girl's boyfriend took our boat out to a beautiful little uninhabited island… "Little Tybee". We had been there a number of times. It was a great place to get away and to go shelling. Usually we had this paradise to ourselves. We did on that day.

Always be aware of the tide. If you aren't, you may be left high and dry…stranded! We laid anchor. I felt we anchored in a safe place about forty feet from shore. When we returned we found the boat high and dry. We were indeed stranded. The tide was constant. We had two extra hours on paradise that day. The tide moves at its' own rate. The boyfriend was very late to work and I was in trouble again. Remember constant!

Have you ever left yourself high and dry because of a bad decision? Have you ever left another person high and dry? Have you ever felt left high and dry by another person? Have you ever felt left high and dry by God? It's a natural feeling. Remember. "Lord, why have you forsaken me?"

The testimony of the faithful is rather clear. "He has never forsaken me"…"He has never given up on me"…"No, in all these things we are more than conquerors through him who loved us"…"There is nothing in all creation that will ever be able to separate us from the love of God in Christ Jesus our Lord"…"Father, into your hands I commit my spirit."

Father, we thank you for the gifts of coastlands, and for the gift of tides. Lord, we thank you for the gift of your faithfulness and your constant love. We confess that we have been stranded spiritually. Give us grace to be numbered with the faithful and empower us to be open to your presence and your touch. In the name of the one who is constant. Amen.

The Dragonfly's Compass

"As the deer pants for streams of water, so my soul pants for you, O God. My soul thirsts for God, for the living God." – Psalm 42:1-2 (NIV)

It was fascinating...a squadron of dragonflies in flight. This almost became a daily sighting on the marsh. We had a very wet summer and a mild winter. Conditions seemed to have been just right for an overabundance in the insect world. Individually, dragonflies shot off in all different directions, up, down, sideways...at all kinds of angles, but corporately, as one body, they seem to move in the same general direction.

Scientists believe that dragonflies have built-in compasses, similar to migratory birds. They have discovered, with the aid of very tiny transmitters attached to these skillful fliers, that if one dragonfly gets off course, the compass within brings him or her back to the correct course. It is still a mystery how it all works, but they believe.

There are those who believe that human beings have a built-in compass as well. It is also a mystery, but still they believe.

As a young seminarian, I remember reading these words for the very first time. They struck a chord in my soul then and still do today. The author wrote in the fourth century. He is Saint Augustine, one of the Fathers of the early church. "You made us for yourself, O Lord, and our heart is restless until it rests in you."

The compass is the Spirit of the Living God, the Spirit of life and love itself testifying with our spirit that "our heart is restless until it rests in you." It is easily denied and often rejected, but still rock solid truth. Jesus says it lovingly and plainly…"I will give you rest", "My peace, I leave with you", "My peace, I give you…."

"My soul pants for you, O God. My soul thirsts for God, the living God."

Dear Father, thank you for the gift of restlessness. Thank you for the gift of the Spirit that testifies with our spirits that our hearts are indeed restless until we rest in you. Thank you, dear Lord, for those who have gone before and who have kept the faith. Jesus, thank you for the compass within. In His holy name. Amen.

Location

"The son said to him, 'Father, I have sinned against heaven and against you, I am no longer worthy to be called your son.'" – Luke 15:21 (NIV)

It was at sunset in mid-February on East Beach. The tide was very low. There was one specific location, one spot where the light from the lighthouse could be seen without the King and Prince Resort completely obstructing the view. Shifting sands had created a new pathway to this particular spot. It was at the water's edge and about a quarter to a half mile out. The light penetrating the darkness was amazing. I stood in silence and in awe.

A young man made his cut and the football landed in his hands. The route called for perfect timing and for perfect location. He was at the right spot, at the right moment. There are those who have found a special location, a spot to experience His light penetrating the darkness and to stand in awe.

"Father, I have sinned...", "Lord, be merciful to me a sinner." The perfect location.

Obstacles and sins are ever present. They are constantly with us. Remember they are a part of the fabric of life. Obstacles and sins obstruct the view, the pathway. They come with the territory. They come in all shapes and sizes.

Still there is a location that clears away all obstacles and all sins. That location, that spot is any place where heartfelt confession is offered. "Father, I have sinned...., I have missed the mark. Be merciful to me a sinner." Acceptance and grace enter in and life is changed. The light of God's love penetrates the darkness in our souls and opens pathways to life full, rich and abundant.

Finding the lighthouse and that location was breathtaking. Finding the location where my confessions are given is sacramental. Where is your location? He provides the light and the love. That's His business; His deepest desire!

Father God, thank you for lighthouses and for light. Thank you for those locations where we find in our darkest hours the light of hope and love, your redemptive action. Father, thank you for those words Jesus spoke so long ago and still speaks today..."I am the light of the world; he who follows me will not walk in darkness, but will have the light of life." In the name of the one who offers life. Amen.

"Do You Believe...?"

"The virgin will be with child and will give birth to a son, and they will call him Emmanuel"----which means, "God with us." – Matthew 1:23 (NIV)

"Do you believe...?" He used his BIG TOE to inscribe his message in the sand. The big toe thing was new for me. He had a good big toe. My initial thoughts were a marriage proposal, or maybe a much needed apology. He was on the beach near the King and Prince, I could see him bringing her down for a walk and letting her see the message and popping the question, or asking for forgiveness. He continued, "Do you believe in m...." Aye, I said "in me?" I was wrong. He concluded with his toe, "Do you believe in magic? Love is magic!" I took photographs at that moment. I was impressed. Now, I waited to see him turn toward the King and Prince and to bring her down for that walk, but to my surprise he went in the opposite direction toward the Coast Guard Station. His sand script was for anyone who took the time to stop and read.

"Do you believe?" "Sure!" The answer is naturally "Yes." Each of us have treasured beliefs. Everyone believes in something or someone! Our beliefs guide and lead us. It's a great question, even an eternal one.

Life demands an answer.

"For God so loved the world that he gave his one and only Son, that whoever believes in him shall not perish, but have eternal life." (John 3:16) "God is love." (I John 4:8)

"Let not your hearts be troubled. Believe in God; believe also in me. In my Father's house are many mansions; if it were not so, I would have told you. I go to prepare a place for you. And if I go and prepare for you, I will come again, and receive you unto myself; that where I am, there you may be also." (John 14:1-3)
"The virgin will be with child and will give birth to a son, and they will call him Emmanuel which means "God with us." (Matthew 1:23)

Yes, our beliefs are ultimately eternal!

Dear Father, thank you for the gift of belief. Thank you for all those who have gone before in faith. Lord, thank you for those who inscribed belief in you in our hearts and in our souls. Empower us to join their number and inscribe belief in you in others. In the name of Emmanuel..."God with us." Amen.

"Do you believe?"

The King and Prince/Massengale Park.

Home

"For we know that if the earthly tent we live in is destroyed, we have a building from God, a house not made with hands, eternal in the heavens." – II Corinthians 5:1 (RSV)

It was late in the day. He was walking with his mom on the Boardwalk. I called him Johnny! The sun would be down in thirty minutes or less. They were headed home. Johnny was three, maybe four at most. He turned and took one last look at the beach…that wonderful beach. Obviously, it had been a great day. I saw that yearning in his eye. I had known that yearning as well, "not now, not yet." The beach was not finished with my young friend. The beach still called to him softly and tenderly…"come to me." In the twinkling of an eye, Johnny changed his momentum and direction. He headed back. Truly, the beach had him hook, line and sinker. His mom almost had to tackle him to continue their trek home.

Then God spoke in silence, "How about you, my child? How many times have you been pulled from home by yearnings in your own spirit?" Yearnings that promised good, but more often than not failed to deliver. Make no mistake, there are valued yearnings that do deliver the promised good. There is no question about the beach delivering good. Ask Johnny! Ask me!

Still our Heavenly Father promises ultimate good… home. In home, He offers joy that only can be found in a relationship with Him. The Father of all creation promises a peace that the world will never comprehend or understand.

Jesus gives us a home, not made with hands...eternal in the heavens. He provides us with a home on earth and in heaven where acceptance, love, mercy, and grace live. How many times have I allowed myself to be wooed from home?

Johnny, be careful young friend. Enjoy the beach. It is truly a gift of God. Remember the one who created the beach and also the ultimate good...home. He will not tackle us. We must decide which yearnings we will follow! "We have a building from God, not made with hands...eternal."

Father God, we thank you for the gift of home and for relationships of love, joy, and peace. Thank you for wooing us. Thank you for never giving up on us. Jesus, give us grace and wisdom, as we seek to woo others into a home not made with hands. In the name of the one who still provides home. Amen.

Week Seven

"You yourselves have seen what I did to Egypt, and how I carried you on eagles' wings and brought you to myself."
– Exodus19:4 (NIV)

Stormy Days Are a Certainty

"He got up, rebuked the wind and said to the waves, 'Quiet! Be still!' Then the wind died down and it was completely calm." – Mark 4:39 (NIV)

By the sea, some days are filled with peace, calm, stillness and serenity. Again by the sea, some days are filled with fear, turbulence, uneasiness, and anxiety.

It was another Northeaster. The waves were violently beating against the pier and the Johnson Rocks, even over the rocks in some places. Sea water was in the street. Storm clouds had formed and in the distance, lighting flashed brightly and great claps of thunder were heard. The rain was headed toward landfall. The storm was coming rapidly. Strong winds blew against my body. It was noisy and disconcerting.

Then Jesus said to the wind and waves, "Quiet! Be still." And they were!

How many times have we joined with the disciples and asked, "Do you care?" They asked that of Jesus. "Teacher, don't you care if we drown?" How many times have we asked that question?

Some of our days are very similar to that day on the Sea of Galilee. There have always been storms. They come in many shapes and sizes. They have the power to break the peace, the calm, the stillness, and the serenity. Fear lives and grows stronger by the moment. It is like a small cancer cell. It begins slowly, but it grows rapidly and constantly.

Still Jesus comes! Does He understand the storms that come to us? Does He care about us? Does He have any power over our storms? Again, does He understand?

Remember His words in the midst of His own storm, "Father into your hands I commit my spirit." Remember His word to the thief…"Today, you will be with me in paradise."

Lord, grant that we might hear your questions to us with love. "Why are you so afraid? Do you still have no faith?" Father, thank you for never giving up on us. Lord, empower us to join others in giving thanks to you! In the name of the one who still calms the storm within. Amen.

The "Hand Talker"

"But what about you?" he asked. "Who do you say I am?"
Peter answered, "The Christ of God." – Luke 9:20 (NIV)

It was a clear day in November; the temp was thirty-nine degrees with a steady northeast wind. The tide was extremely low. There was a large beach, but not many people. I saw in the distance this lone figure coming from the north at a very good pace. The individual seemed to be exercising arms as well. Coming closer, I determined she was not intentionally exercising her arms, she was talking on her phone. She was a "hand talker." She was totally focused and very energetic. Her hands were moving all over the place.

"Tie his hands behind him and he would not be able to talk." I have been labeled a "hand talker" on a number of occasions. I need my hands when I talk. Are you a "hand talker"? Do you know anyone who is?

Moses seems to be a "hand talker." They are making their way out of Egypt and he is up front leading with words and hands. As they come to the Red Sea and make the crossing, again Moses offers encouragement with words and hands. You see it again and again. David is a "hand talker" as well. After that great victory, David leads his warriors and his people into Jerusalem with singing and dancing. In battle, he was a "hand talker." Warriors by necessity are "hand talkers."

And then there is Peter. He is quick to speak and very quick to act. "You are the Christ of God." I see in my mind's eye, Peter speaking and pointing to Jesus with love…"You are…." He is filled with energy and enthusiasm. Remember in the garden, he speaks and lifts his hand.

Like Peter, you and I have a message to share…"The Christ of God." Some of us are "hand talkers" and some are not. Both are needed, even called, and clearly commissioned. May our energy and our enthusiasm affirm again and again "The Christ."

Lord God, we thank you for "The Christ." Jesus, we thank you for all those who made the great affirmation in our faith journey and helped to make the difference for us. Forgive us when we fail to remember our callings. Empower us to make the difference as well, in this day and this hour. In His holy name. Amen.

The Journey

"And he said to them, 'Follow me....'"
– Matthew 4:19 (RSV)

Thirteen! Not my favorite number, but that morning on the beach, in a twenty to thirty minute time frame, I counted thirteen jet streams. That was a high for me. I have been told there is an airway in the sky known as the coastal corridor. We live under that corridor. It is not an unusual thing to see jet streams from the beach. They are treasures by the sea!

I often think about the people on those jets. At times, my prayers are offered for them. All are on the journey, just as we are. We are all at different places on that journey. Some are walking on the mountain top...celebrating the union of a young couple, or celebrating the birth of a grandchild. A young soldier returning safely from another tour of duty in Iraq is giving thanks to God for the United States of America and for her home. Another is walking on the mountain top after landing that dream job.

Still others are walking in the valley of darkness. A marriage has ended in bitter divorce. A family gathers in the clouds of grief and great pain...death has arrived too early for a young college student. A young soldier prepares for that first tour in a war zone with prayer and thoughts of his home and his loved ones. Another is walking in the valley of darkness after losing that dream job of twenty-seven years. We are at different places at any given moment on this journey.

125

"Follow me!" Jesus understands my journey! He understands yours. His invitation is to all. "Come to me, all you who are weary and burdened, I will give your rest." "Follow me!" "I have come that you might have life and have it more abundantly." "Follow me!" "I will make you fishers of men." He understands the need for purpose, meaning and value in life. We need to make a difference! "Follow me!" "I will never leave you, I will never forsake you!" "Follow me!" We are loved, all of us!

Father God, thank you for the journey. Thank you for your holy presence and your tender touch on the mountain and in the valley. Lord Jesus, thank you for your invitation to "follow." Jesus, we lift to you all who are on the journey. Father, may we be listed among the ones who encourage brothers and sisters to "follow." In His holy name. Amen.

One jet stream but hundreds of souls and precious stories.

An early morning hour from the King and Prince.

"Dancing Waters"

"...a time to weep and a time to laugh, a time to mourn and a time to dance..."– Ecclesiastes 3:4 (RSV)

"Dancing water?" Where can I get this "dancing water?" Go to the beach in the morning hour! Wear a sun visor. It occurs when light from the sun touches water from the earth. "Dancing water" occurs when heaven and earth touch. It's rhythmic, graceful, calming, refreshing, renewing and easily missed. Slow down. Look with heart and soul. Watch a wave begin to form and catch a glimpse of the "dancing waters." Continue to watch the wave crest and break. Observe carefully the foam as it moves landward. Remember, slow down! It's easily missed!

There is a time to weep and a time to mourn. "Jesus wept!" Tears are gifts given to release and to express our deepest emotion...love. Never deny grief. We are designed with tear ducts. Weeping and mourning are natural. Cry until you can cry no more. It is hard to believe, but it happens.

There is also a time to laugh and a time to dance. When the heart of God touches the heart of man, there is rejoicing, celebrating, laughing and dancing.

Jesus put it very simply. There was dancing, laughing, rejoicing, and celebrating, when the Prodigal Son returned home. There is more joy in heaven over one sinner who repents. Dancing in heaven, can you see it? Jesus wept, but I also know He danced as well. Why? Because of the victory, we have in Him! Love wins! "Believe in God." "I will never

129

leave you!" "My peace, I give to you." Paul writes, "Rejoice in the Lord always. I will say it again, rejoice!" Celebrate! Laugh! Dance!

The next time you go to the beach, look for "dancing water." Remember it is easily missed. Slow down! I hope you do a little dancing yourself, if not physically…at least spiritually. I have done each! Love wins! Victory is assured!

Father God, thank you for sunlight and for water; "dancing water." Lord, thank you for the gift of tears and for the gift of dance. Jesus, thank you for your victory. Daily, empower us to be open to that victory and to the reality that love wins. Dear Lord, empower us to celebrate, to laugh, to rejoice, and yes, to dance. In the name of the one who gives us tears and gives us dancing. Amen.

Be very careful to watch with thanksgiving and joy, dancing waters.

Stewards

"This is how one should regard us, as servants of Christ and stewards of the mysteries of God. Moreover, it is required of stewards that they be found trustworthy."
– I Corinthians 4:1-2 (RSV)

We had a long hard rain the night before. It did produce a good night's sleep. The sand was smooth. I had just said again, "Lord, I'm listening." Shortly after that I looked down and saw an old rusty fish hook. I thought about a toddler and the damage that could be done. Think about it. I also thought about a barefooted teen-ager and again the damage. I can understand a fish hook. Fishermen often lose hooks.

I have a much harder time understanding aluminum cans, tin ones, bottles, broken ones, Styrofoam cups, plastic ones, paper plates, and the list goes on. I have a thing called temper. I have the potential of becoming angry, sad, discouraged, and even apathetic. Does it bother you? God has blessed us with such great natural beauty. The coastlands do not hold the market on beauty. The Father has been gracious again and again.

"Lord, what are you saying?" "Be a good steward. Encourage good stewardship. Remember the Father's world is a precious and holy gift."

We have some friends from Germany, who walk the same route we walk. They usually have a Wal-Mart bag and a pair of long handled tweezers. He picks up litter. She carries the bag.

We have a choice. We can complain or commit. We can be apathetic or active. We can be discouragers or encouragers. Why should we pick up after one who fails to care? Our German friends are committed. They are active encouragers.

Now what did I do with that Wal-Mart bag? By the way, I did pick up the old rusty fish hook and made a fresh new commitment!

Father, thank you for the natural beauty of the Earth. Thank you for those who have gone before and were worthy stewards. Forgive us when we fail to commit. Give us grace and wisdom to enjoy the beauty and to care for it. In the name of the one who cares for His creation. Amen.

Change

"No, in all these things we are more than conquerors through him who loved us. For I am sure that neither death, nor life, nor angels, nor principalities, nor things present, nor things to come, nor powers, nor height, nor depth, nor anything in all creation will be able to separate us from the love of God in Christ Jesus our Lord." – Romans 8:37-39 (RSV)

Change is assured. The beach is constantly changing. Tide, wind, rain, and people all contribute to an ever-changing beach. Sunday morning, a northeast wind, with help from the tide, had cut a three foot drop-off on the beach in the sand. In less than twelve hours, a dramatic change had taken place. In that early morning darkness, it was difficult finding a place to jump down to get to the water's edge. I had never seen this much change before.

Usually change comes in slower increments, but it still comes. It is assured. That's the nature of the beach. Some changes are not even noticeable, but are still present. For many a beachcomber, these changes add to the mystery and to the beauty of the beach. Every day is fresh and new. Yesterday will not be like today. Tomorrow will not be like yesterday. Two things remain constant for the beach-comber...the sun and the tide.

Life is filled with change. When changes cease, life ceases. Sometimes the change is traumatic. It happens in an instant, in the twinkling of an eye, in a heartbeat. Most changes in life are like changes at the beach. Many take place unnoticed. One day, we look around and things are not the same…life changes. Like the beach, many factors come into play.

Paul wrote to the Romans and shared what the Lord so graciously had shared with him. Paul's conviction was that when life changes and we are not in control, we have a constant. That constant is the love of the living Lord…His tender touch. "I will not leave you."

Lord, thank you for the gift of life. Father, thank you for the one who is the same, yesterday, today and forever. Thank you for the promise. Lord, when we face change and find ourselves not in control, help us to remember that through your love, we are more than conquerors. In the name of the one who offers love that is constant and everlasting. Amen.

The Bald Eagle

"You yourselves have seen what I did to Egypt, and how I carried you on eagles' wings and brought you to myself."
– Exodus19:4 (RSV)

Normally on Sundays I sing hymns of faith, often aloud or on occasion meditatively. On this day, I was not singing. I had a bad case of the mulligrubs. Do you understand what I mean? It's a form of grumbling or complaining, etc.

My focus was our beloved nation: foreclosures, bankruptcies, unemployment, etc. There is a general decay in our national fabric morally, physically, spiritually, etc. Like I said, "a bad case." Greed is alive and well. Credit seems to be king. The rich become richer. The poor become poorer. The great divide continues to grow. Have you ever had similar thoughts?

Then I made my turn toward home. You know my mood. There was a strong wind coming out of the south. And then it happened! I have been on the beach at least three thousand plus times. I have been saddened and uplifted by sights I have seen. I have never seen anything more magnificent or glorious. A bald eagle landed 20 yards in front of me. That's right…a bald eagle! I saw him gently touchdown…beautiful. I stopped in my tracks. He took my breath away.

Then these words came to my spirit. "I have carried you on eagles' wings," as a nation and as an individual. Then these words to Moses came. "I am who I am." Then the words of Jesus came. "I am the door… the way… the truth… the light." The message was "I am who I am" is still in charge. The call is to honor Him.

I knew when I took my next step, he would take flight. He did! It was a sight to behold. The winds lifted him skyward, overwhelming! And then I saw the flag, "Old Glory." It was tattered, torn, and frayed, but it was flying. Then these words came. "You have a choice, Jim. You can mulligrub or you can fly. You can sit on the sidelines or you can get on the field. What will it be? The choice is yours!"

"I am who I am," thank you. Thank you for your holy gift of life. Thank you for your desire and your power to lift us up on eagles' wings. Father, thank you for the gift of freedom. Dear Jesus, thank you for "the door, the way, the truth and the light." Forgive us when we grumble and complain. Empower us to open ourselves to you and fly. In His holy name. Amen.

Old Glory at the Coast Guard Station.

Week Eight

"And after the fire came a gentle whisper. When Elijah
heard it, he pulled his cloak over his face…" Then a voice
said to him, "What are you doing here, Elijah?"
– I Kings 19:12b-13 (NIV)

Take Flight

"Love the Lord your God with all your heart and with all soul and with all your mind...love your neighbor as yourself." – Matthew 22: 37, 39 (NIV)

I was on my morning bike ride by the marsh, headed to the beach, deep in thought...not really in the present. Have you ever been there...not in the present? Then it happened. I saw him out of the corner of my eye. He was less than ten feet from me. He startled me and I startled him. I have never been that close to one. The Great Blue Heron took flight at that moment. It was magnificent! His take off was a thing of pure grace and awesome beauty. I have joyfully relived that encounter a number of times.

God desires that we take flight spiritually. Listen as He gives Moses these eternal words on Mount Sinai..."You yourselves have seen what I did to Egypt, and how I carried you on eagles' wings and brought you to myself." Clearly we hear Jesus... "I have come to set the prisoner free...."

The Great Blue Heron is not bound to this earth and neither are we.

I saw "Miss Becky" take flight spiritually on many occasions. I was her pastor for almost eight years. She was a registered nurse and her husband, George, was a pharmacist. They were never able to have children. They found their children in God's family, the church. She taught the Kindergarten and First Grade Sunday School Class for thirty plus years. George lovingly supported her efforts. Each Sunday, with love she took flight and shared what she had freely received. She encouraged taking flight, not only with words, but also with deeds. Our daughters adopted her to be their Godmother. At an early age, they learned from her about taking flight. She is now taking flight on the other side. Thanks be to God.

How did she do that? How do we? By His amazing grace, and by walking in His holy way, "Love the Lord your God…and love your neighbor as yourself."

Take flight, my brother! Take flight, my sister!

Father God, thank you for the gift of flight. May we soar on the wings of your grace. Give us wings to share what we have so freely received. In His holy name. Amen.

Taking flight.

Urging – A Gentle Whisper

"And after the fire came a gentle whisper. When Elijah heard it, he pulled his cloak over his face..." Then a voice said to him, "What are you doing here, Elijah?"
– I Kings 19:12b-13 (NIV)

Urgings are commonplace. Sometimes they are ignored. Other times they are obeyed. Over the years, I have known those who have been obedient to what they felt were urgings from the Lord of a gentle whisper. I have heard testimonies of holy encounters, divine affirmations and stronger directions. Elijah finally listened to that urging... to that gentle whisper and life changed.

She was obedient to that urging in her own spirit.

This is her story. Our friend is a gifted photographer. This artist with a camera understands color, light and angles. She is patient and persistent. She is consistently in pursuit of excellence. This lady is another treasure hunter, in search of visual beauty. Often Lou combs the beach and also the island with the eye of an eagle, looking for just the right treasure.

On this particular day, she found herself surrounded by a cluster of magnificent trees. It was early morning, when she saw the sunlight filtered through the trees. She had taken several shots. She was about to leave and had an urging to take just one more. She aimed her camera toward the sunlight and took one more.

From the naked eye, she saw only the sunlight filtered through the cluster of trees, nothing out of the ordinary, but peaceful and calming. After the shot had been processed and she had seen it for the first time, she remembered the urging and her obedience and was overwhelmed by what she saw.

The finished photograph had captured the trees, the sunlight, and to her amazement, a cross radiating out from the filtered light, an extraordinary gift for the one who obeyed. It was truly a blessing for her.

Father of the gentle whisper, thank you for the gift of urging. Jesus, teach us to be open, to be alive, to be obedient. Lord, empower us to receive your urgings day by day. In the name of the one who still whispers with grace, kindness and gentleness. Amen.

On A Clear Day

"We live by faith, not by sight." – II Corinthians 5:7 (NIV)

Have you ever walked a beach? Have you ever walked East Beach on Saint Simons Island? Have you ever sighted Cumberland Island from there? It's one of the treasures I seek to find almost daily.

It was a clear day…cold…in the mid-thirties, with strong wind gusts coming out of the south. Cumberland is due south, approximately ten miles. On a clear day, when it is not too hazy, you will find this treasure right on the edge of the horizon. I saw Cumberland that cold morning…like a glittering emerald.

Not all days are clear. Some are dark. Others are hazy. Still others are cloudy. Some are foggy. It was a foggy morning. Visibility was limited to about twenty feet. There was no sighting of Cumberland on that particular day. Still, after finding my bearings I could point toward that jewel on the horizon. How? Because of sight, I had seen it before and knew where it was.

Thomas said, "Unless I see…I will not believe it." Jesus replied, "Blessed are those who have not seen and yet have believed." Paul writes, "We live by faith, not by sight."

A clear day became dark in a split second. He was twelve and ready for a very active summer. The doctor said, "Polio". Within hours, he was in a polio hospital. It was thought to be very contagious and even deadly.

The darkness continued to grow. Fear filled his heart and his spirit. The prayer was simple, but from deep down within, "Lord, I'm afraid." Shortly after that, he was given a peace. He knew in his heart that he was not alone. The Lord was present and would never forsake him. The word is faith. I was that boy.

The next time you are on East Beach, sight Cumberland… remember by faith, not by sight.

Father, thank you for clear days. Thank you for faith. Jesus, thank you for a living, loving relationship that still penetrates the darkest hour. Forgive us when we fail to exercise faith. Lord, empower us to share what we have been freely given. In name of the Father, the Son and the Holy Spirit. Amen.

The Cicadas' Symphony

"Enter his gates with thanksgiving and his courts with praise; give thanks to him and praise his name."
– Psalm 100:4 (NIV)

It was a typical hot humid day in August, although summer had not been typical. We had an abundance of rain, all the yards and all the plants were very healthy and green. Normally, it is much drier. There was a gentle breeze on our backs, as we rode our bikes by the marsh headed home.

We were about to make our final turn, then it happened. The cicadas, as if they were following a conductor, seemed to come in all together on his down beat. The chord was struck and music filled the air. It was magnificent, glorious and awe inspiring. It was a God moment…nature's symphony at its best. I believe Beethoven would have said, "Yes."

Music is in our DNA. There is evidence of music dating back to the beginning of recorded history. In ancient Egypt, 4,000 B.C., harps and flutes filled the air with music. Today, the airwaves are filled with music. Without music, there would be a big hole in life. There are those who believe it is a God-given gift. Music comforts, challenges, encourages, points, uplifts, inspires, corrects, sets free, makes whole, brings redemption and offers celebration.

No doubt, the highest form of music is praise.

John Wesley's Directions for Singing, VII. "Above all sing spiritually. Have an eye to God in every word you sing. Aim at pleasing him more than yourself, or any other creature...."

When the created offers praise and thanksgiving to the Creator, when the redeemed offers heart and soul through music to the Redeemer, and when the ones who walked in great darkness lift voices in praise to the one who offered and still offers eternal light, love, joy, and peace reign. "Praise him! Praise him!"

Father, thank you for the Holy gift of your redeeming love and of praise and worship. Thank you for all those who gather to lift voices in praise to you and to your Son. Thank you for those voices that may crack, but still with heart and soul lift voices in praise. Thank you for love, joy and peace. In His holy name. Amen.

Sunscreen and Protection

"Every Word of God proves true. He is a shield to all who come to him for protection." – Proverbs 30:5 (NLT)

Sun, beach and water are wonderful gifts, but can be dangerous and even deadly.

They had just arrived on East Beach. The mom's first action was the sunscreen drill. She lathered up the lotion in her hands and began carefully placing it over the bodies of her two girls. She was fully aware of the dangers and the negative consequences of a day at the beach without protection. With just a little more observation, the sunscreen drill was repeated up and down the beach again and again. The message was very clear. We need protection from harmful and sometimes unseen deadly rays.

Life, love and freedom are everlasting holy gifts, but can also be dangerous and deadly.

Each Sunday, this mom arrived with others, as her children headed to be with friends and to be in Sunday School. Music was a part of their life together. "Jesus Loves Me" was one of their favorites. They heard the stories of faith, hope, love and freedom. Stories that had been passed down through the ages. Her children were valued. They were loved. They were treasured. Prayers were lifted in thanksgiving at home and in church. This mom was fully aware of the dangers of life and freedom, and the need for protection. For her, God was her shield and her protection. Jesus was her friend. She prayed for and desired the same for her family. Look around, there were and are others like her.

"The wise woman builds her house, but with her own hands the foolish one tears hers down." (Proverbs 14:1) Who were the wise women? Who were the ones who valued and loved? Who were the ones who built homes recognizing the need for shield and protection? Who were the ones who recognized the need for an everlasting friendship?

Father, thank you for your holy gifts; sun, beach, water, life, love and freedom. Thank you for being our shield, our protection and our everlasting friend. Lord, where we have failed you, forgive us and give wisdom to move forward with courage and faith. In the name of Jesus Christ. Amen.

Tunnel Vision

"Come, see a man who told me all that I ever did. Can this be the Christ?" – John 4:29 (NIV)

I cooled off after my morning run. I had lifted prayers of thanksgiving, confession, intercession, and petition. I confess to you that on that day I was consumed with tunnel vision. It happens. Although I was on the beach physically...I totally missed it spiritually. Mentally, I was not living in the moment. I was somewhere in the past, or in the future, but clearly not in the moment. Have you ever experienced tunnel vision?

There were not very many people out, but there was one gentleman who gently pulled me out of my tunnel vision. He offered a friendly witness. "Did you see the dolphins?" I had not. I looked toward the water and there they were in all their glory...playful, beautiful, magnificent. The dolphins were swift and graceful. They moved through the water with what seemed to be great ease. They have always been amazing to watch. I stopped in my tracks and watched with pure joy and peace. It was an awesome show. It only lasted about three to four minutes, but they were valued minutes.

I lost my tunnel vision with a gentle invitation..."Did you see the dolphins?" I was now living in the moment. Again, Jesus Christ opened the door through one of His children...a total stranger. He was definitely living in the moment.

"Come, see a man...." I wonder if the woman at the well

151

had tunnel vision. I'm confident she did. But now she calls out to those who would give her an audience. Living fully in the moment no longer with tunnel vision, she says, "Come, see a man…."

My brother, my sister, "Did you see the dolphins?" "Come, see a man who told me…."

Father, thank you for the gift of dolphins. Lord God, thank you for encouraging words from brothers, sisters and strangers. Lord Jesus, thank you for those who have with word and deed pointed us toward you. Spirit of the living Lord, fill us with the desire to offer the invitation, "Come, see…." In the blessed name of Jesus Christ. Amen.

"Yes"

"For the Son of God, Jesus Christ, who was preached among you by me and Silas and Timothy, was not 'Yes' and 'No,' but in him it has always been 'Yes.' For no matter how many promises God has made, they are 'Yes' in Christ."
– II Corinthians 1:19-20 (NIV)

Temptations come…tempted to be consumed by the "NO" in life.

It was a cloudy, windy and rainy day on the beach. The wind and rain came out of the north. The tide was low. The rain gently fell on my shoulders and back. My baseball cap kept the rain off my glasses. The hooded jacket kept me dry and comfortable. I was prepared for this moment.

Sandpipers joined me on this morning walk. They seemed to celebrate. Offshore on a sandbar, other sea fowl were nestled tightly together. We were the only ones on the beach. No one was in sight. It was one of those holy moments, when I found myself in blissful solitude.

I heard the soft sound of the rain on my hood and the waves breaking on the shore. And they came. The words came out with the loudest shout I could muster. "YES, LORD! YES! THANK YOU, LORD! YES!" It was one of those "YES" MOMENTS! "YES, LORD! YES!" I held nothing back. On this cloudy, windy and rainy day, I celebrated.

I celebrated with my feathered friends. I celebrated the magnificence of God's creation. I rejoiced in the beauty of the moment. I receive the wonder of His awesome grace and mercy flooding my soul afresh. I celebrated His Spirit testifying with my spirit that I was His child. I am a child of God. I celebrated the "YES" Jesus offers in every moment of every day. I rejoiced in the greatest "YES" of all times and every age. "Father into your hands I commit my spirit." "YES, LORD! YES! THANK YOU, LORD."

Father, thank you for the need we have to celebrate and to affirm the truth…the "Yes" within. Father God, thank you for understanding the temptation to be consumed by the "No." Lord, give us power and wisdom to share the "Yes" moments. Jesus, thank you for the greatest "Yes." "Father, into your hands we commit our spirits." Amen.

Week Nine

"When I consider your heavens, the work of your
fingers, the moon and stars, which you have set in
place, what is man that you are mindful of him,
the son of man that you care for him?"

– Psalm 8:3 (NIV)

Skimming or Crashing

"Come to me, all you who labor and are heavy laden, and I will give you rest." – Matthew 11:28 (RSV)

The pelican skimmed just above the water with beauty and grace. He flowed along on the winds of the morning without effort. My pelican friend floated on the invisible wings of the Creator of this universe. He was surrounded by the magnificence of life. It was truly a majestic sighting. He was guided by another. Our friend was truly blessed. The pelican seemed to rejoice in the moment. He seemed to relish in it. This scene is repeated along the coast day after day, often unnoticed.

Are we good skimmers? Often I crash...never a thing of beauty or grace. From time to time, we are surrounded by winds of change. These winds usually come from our invisible tomorrows. We are not in control, although we tend to believe we are. We seek to be in control. Winds of change always call for the best, but the best is not in me. Again, often I fall short. I am more inclined to complain than to rejoice. Where is the Creator of this universe? Where is my God? Why have you forsaken me? Rather than skim, I crash.

Through the Spirit I understand to be God's Spirit, the Spirit of the living Lord, my friend the pelican gently reminded me that we have one who is eager to give rest and peace. He is eager to teach us how to skim and not crash. He is eager to show us how to float on the winds of the morning. He is eager to empower us, so that we too, might rejoice in the moment and relish in it.

We have a choice. We can crash or we can skim. We can seek to be in control or allow another to be in control... one who fully understands about skimming and living life to its fullest. We can continue to condemn ourselves for crashing again and again, or we can come to trust in one who offers power to lift us upward and surround us with His beauty and His majesty. We can be guided by another. "Come to me...."

Lord, thank you for your beauty and your majesty. Father, thank you for your Son, Jesus Christ. Thank you for your gift of rest and peace. Help us to be open to you and put our complete trust in you. Lord, empower us to rejoice in the moment. In the name of Jesus, who still offers rest to those who willingly come. Amen.

Skimming

Trusting

The Wind

"Now the Lord is the Spirit, and where the Spirit of the Lord is, there is freedom." – II Corinthians 3:17 (NIV)

On the beach, when things are in order, one of the first things that usually happens for me is to determine the direction of the wind. It's nice to have the wind behind your back at the beginning of your beach walk. It's easier than having the wind in your face. The wind helps to set a faster pace. Ask any pilot who flies those crafts above... who create those beautiful jet streams, about a good tail wind. Take a ride on a bike. The wind behind your back is most beneficial. It's freeing.

When the turn is made for the homeward trek, the wind is in your face. On hot and sweaty days, that wind in your face feels refreshing and even uplifting. I have felt it many times. On some very windy days, the wind holds you up... keeps you from falling. Again it's freeing.

"Where the Spirit of the Lord is, there is freedom."

Remember beginning the journey with the Lord? How many years ago? Then as now, our number one aim must always be to determine His direction and walk in it. I took that first step years ago with Him behind my back. He has never left me. I on the other hand from time to time have left Him. But when I know He has my back, I am free! Do you understand? "There is freedom!!"

And when the homeward trek begins and the "Spirit of the

161

Lord" is in your face, He is refreshing and uplifting! He has held me up and kept me from falling many times. I am free! "There is freedom!!"

The next time you make your way to the beach, or step foot in your yard, remember the direction of the wind and the direction of the Lord. Remember, "Freedom."

Father God, thank you for the precious gift of another day. Thank you for the wonderful gift of the wind. Thank you for your desire to be with us and to bless us. Jesus, thank you for being behind us and in front of us. Thank you for the Spirit of the Lord and the holy gift of freedom. Thank you for the awesome gift of your assurance. Lord, empower us to be faithful to your direction, to be joyful in obedience, and to be hopeful in service. In the name of Jesus Christ! Amen.

The Best You Have

"Therefore, my beloved brethren, be steadfast, immovable, always abounding in the work of the Lord, knowing that in the Lord your labor is not in vain."
– I Corinthians 15:58 (RSV)

There was his footprint in the sand. He had been running heavy. He had been pounding the beach very hard. He had left a deep footprint. He was running on his toes. I rarely do that now. His stride was very long. I could not come close to his distance. He must have been a tall, strong young man. Whenever I looked down, I saw his stride. It was frustrating.

Throughout my morning run, his stride was constantly present. I tried my best to make his stride. It was impossible. No way. Thank you Lord, for another treasure by the sea.

We can easily become frustrated, blue, depressed, because we are limited. Most of us have known those feelings. We can even become angry with God, with others, and with ourselves. We can live in denial and cover up what we feel. We can just not play the game... not even come to bat!

We can't stride like some can. Each of us can make a list of those things we can't do. I can't sing like Bill Gaither. I can't write like Philip Yancey. I can't preach like Billy Graham. I can't give like...

Thank God, the Lord knows our hearts. He knows our desires. He knows when we offer the best we have to the

163

highest we know. We are instructed to love the Lord with all our hearts, our minds, our souls and our strength and to love our neighbor as ourselves.

God's focus is not on our brother's stride, but on ours. Why should my focus be on others? What am I offering? Am I ready to take the best stride I have for Christ, remembering always that it is not in vain?

Lord, thank you for the fact that the only shoes we need to fill are our own. Father, give us grace and strength to take strides worthy of the one who offers all He has. Empower us to be "steadfast, immovable, always abounding...." In the name of the one who knows all about footprints in the sand and in life. Amen.

Keep your focus, remember the best you have.

Spiritual Warmth

"When I consider your heavens, the work of your fingers, the moon and stars, which you have set in place, what is man that you are mindful of him, the son of man that you care for him?" – Psalm 8:3 (NIV)

It was January on Saint Simons Island. The sun was about to awake another day. I was hopeful that I hadn't miss it. I completed my beach run with my back to the breaking light. I turned toward the light and stopped. The sun began its slow, but steady climb. It was not missed! It seemed to come out of the depths of the sea. It looked almost liquid. The sun took less than three minutes to clear the horizon. There was not a cloud in the sky. The morning was very cold. No one was in sight. The morning sun brought warmth to a body that desired warmth. It felt refreshing and renewing.

Another treasure by the sea was received. I was blessed again by the one who made the heavens and the earth, by the one who set the moon and stars in place, and yes, by the one who understood all of my questions.

It was a Christ moment. Christ was present indeed! With love, He reminded me of my own need to consider the heavens, and the work of His fingers. He reminded me of my own question, "Lord, who am I that you care for me?"

Each new morning, we receive invitations. "Cast all your anxieties on Him, for He cares for you." "Come to me... and I will give you rest." "My peace, I give to you; not as the world gives...." "I will not leave you...." "I will never forsake you...."

As the sun warms the body physically, we need to remember that Jesus Christ, the Son of God, desires spiritually to warm our hearts and souls with light, love, peace and joy. In each case, we must make the turn toward the warmth. By His everlasting grace, we must be open mentally and spiritually to His invitation and to His gentle touch.

Father, thank you for the gift of care. Thank you for the warmth of the sun and the gift of another sunrise. Father, as we turn toward the sun for physical warmth, may we be led to turn toward you for spiritual warmth. Lord, help us encourage others to be open to your invitation...to your warmth and touch. In the name of the one who says, "Come to me...." Amen.

Open to physical and spiritual warmth.

Christmas and Hidden Dangers

"And she gave birth to her first-born son and wrapped him in swaddling cloths, and laid him in a manager..."
– Luke 2:7 (RSV)

There are hidden, unseen dangers in the marsh. I enjoy the marsh. It's beautiful. The wind blows and the marsh grasses dance in unison. The marsh can calm a soul, and bless a spirit. It is one of God's gracious gifts. I love the sounds of the marsh, even the smells.

It was in Advent...leading to Christmas. It was an early morning hour. There had been heavy dew. That's when I saw one of the hidden, unseen dangers for the very first time. The marsh was not a friendly place for flying insects. It looked very friendly, but it was not! Because of the heavy dew I saw hundreds, no thousands of spider-webs throughout the marsh awaiting their prey! Danger!

There are hidden, unseen dangers in the Christmas season. We treasure Christmas. It's glorious. "Her first-born son" still calms the soul and blesses the spirit. In that season, we are reminded and still remind each other of God's greatest gift to humankind. The sounds and the smells of the season are refreshing and uplifting. Peace, hope, love and joy are offered again and again. His touch is tender and personal.

But, yes, even in Christmas there are hidden, unseen dangers awaiting us. The webs are hidden; unseen...not friendly to humankind. Tinsel and glitter may pull us from the real reason for the season...webs in their own unique way. Christmas lights and Christmas sounds may pull us further away. Parties and busy schedules may also pull. Secularism, commercialism and consumerism have their own particular pull on us. The dangers are alive, but hidden and unseen. The real danger is we can end up with no room in our spirits for the most precious relationship ever offered...a grace relationship with the Son of the living God. Can you identify with any hidden dangers?

Father, thank you for the gift of the marsh, for its beauty. Yes, Lord, and ten billion times over, thank you for the gift of your Son. Empower us to be open to His love and His grace daily...yes, moment by moment. May we be fully aware of the hidden dangers that are very present. May our inns, our hearts and our souls be open to His holy call. In the name of the babe of Bethlehem. Amen.

Footprints and Palm Sunday

"They took palm branches and went out to meet him, shouting, Hosanna!" "Blessed is he who comes in the name of the Lord!" "Blessed is the King of Israel!"
— John 12:13 (NIV)

It was early Sunday morning, before the sunrise. Still there was light...the first light of day. In that morning light, two sets of footprints were easily seen on the beach. Near by a single set was also seen. In the stillness and freshness of the new day, the poem, "Footprints in the Sand" came to my mind and to my spirit.

The author, Mary Stevenson, grew up during the great depression. At the tender age of six, her mother died. Her father became the caregiver for a large family of eight. At the age of sixteen, she wrote the poem. Through the years, she shared handwritten copies with loved ones and friends.

She had a dream and she was with the Lord. There were two sets of footprints in the sand...her prints and His. She was given a vision of her life journey. From time to time, there was just one set of prints in the sand. In her dream, she recognized that when life had been at its darkest and most painful, there was only one set of prints, hers. She wondered why the Lord left her in those dark times and asked Him. His response was "My child, in those times I carried you."

They were on top. "They took palm branches and went out to meet Him..." They were waving the branches. They were shouting. "Hosanna!" "Blessed is He who comes in the name of the Lord." They were filled with faith and hope, thanksgiving and joy. It was definitely a "two footprint" day. They were together at last. The sun was bright and warm. But as the week progressed, the days and nights grew darker and deeply painful. Fear and doubt now ruled, where faith and hope had lived. Betrayed! Arrested! Denied! Stripped! Whipped! Judged! Condemned! "Crucify him!" Crucified! Buried!

Palm Sundays come and go, as do Good Fridays, but He carried His beloved in those darkest of nights and still does today. There is one set of footprints...His!

Thank you, dear Lord for your footprints in the sand. Empower us to be open to your tender loving touch and your footprint next to ours. May we honor you with our footprints. In the name of the Father, the Son, and the Holy Spirit. Amen.

The Christmas Tree

"And now these three remain: faith, hope and love. But the greatest of these is love." – I Corinthians 13:13 (NIV)

The Christmas tree appeared front page center in our local paper, The Brunswick News. It was not the tree from the White House in Washington, D.C., nor from City Hall in Brunswick, nor from The Cloister on Sea Island. It was a beautiful piece of driftwood on East Beach, Saint Simons Island, very near the Coast Guard Station walkover.

A couple of dog walkers began this beach decorating opportunity. They got help from others by moving a sizeable piece of driftwood from the surf beyond the high tide mark. The first ornament was a red ball. From there other beachcombers joined the community effort. More balls were added. Other items were included: tangerines, Coca Cola cans, garlands, shells of all kinds, star fish, sand dollars, dolphins, a shark, a Christmas tree light bulb with the inscription "De Colores", Santa Claus, snowmen, French horns, a wooden soldier, a giraffe, a horseshoe, wreaths, bells, stars, angels, crosses and the list went on. Even a beach chair was added for those who wanted to take a break and enjoy the beauty of God's creation and/or the wonder of a driftwood Christmas tree.

The Christmas tree was a gift and gifts are designed to be shared and experienced with others. That made this particular gift at least for me, holy, even sacramental. It was indeed another treasure by the sea.

171

I felt led to collect some driftwood from the beach and created an offering for the tree, for neighbors, and for Christ. My wife and I made a cross and hung it in place. It was crudely done, but was offered with love. I remembered the words spoken so very long ago. "And now these three remain: faith, hope, and love. But the greatest of these is love." We joined a company of others giving thanks for atoning faith, for everlasting hope and for redeeming love.

Father, as we come to celebrate the birth of your Son, Emmanuel, God with us, once again, we, together, give you thanks. We lift Your name in praise and in thanksgiving. We give thanks for His atoning faith, for His everlasting hope and for His redeeming love. Empower us to receive afresh, what you so eagerly desire to give. In the holy name of Emmanuel. Amen.

The beach community in action.

Grace and love.

Week Ten

"But thanks be to God, who gives us the
victory through our Lord Jesus Christ."
– I Corinthians 15:57 (RSV)

Together

"For where two or three come together in my name, I am there." – Matthew 18:20 (TEV)

The live oaks were majestic. The Spanish moss waved gently at the impulse of the breeze. The grounds were immaculate; the silence welcoming. The breeze was refreshing. This treasure by the Frederica River was revisited afresh. This is a place where it is common practice for two or three or more to come together in His holy name and to experience anew the companion who walks and talks with His own.

The doors of Epworth by the Sea, a Christian Retreat Center, officially opened on July 25, 1950. Over eight hundred souls came together in His name. From the very beginning, the foundation of Epworth has been faith, prayer, vision, love and coming together in His name. Still today, brothers and sisters come together in praise and in worship. They come from across the State of Georgia, the southeast, the nation and the world. They come to meet the companion, who walks and talks with His own. Decisions and commitments have been made with the Lord on these holy grounds. Lives have been redeemed and changed. The call to ministry for laity and clergy has been received and accepted time and time again.

The Frederica River and the Marshes of Glynn at Epworth offer magnificent foregrounds for glorious sunsets. St. Simons Island is noted for her sunsets. There are many sites for experiencing them on the island, across our beloved country, and around this delicate world. A sunset can be a God thing! It can be holy! Please remember His desire is for tender and eternal relationships. Sunsets are beyond compare. No two are alike. Remember He desires to walk and talk with each of us. His relationships are beyond compare as well. No two are alike. Bring a friend, or two. Wait expectantly with patience and with love for the sunset and for the companion. Be gentle with yourself. Remember, "Together." Remember His word, "I am there."

Father God, thank you for the Spirit that lovingly and tenderly woos us to come together in His name. Thank you for the Spirit that testifies with our spirits that we belong to you. We are your children. Thank you, Jesus for the gifts of sunsets and sunrises. Lord, thank you for bringing us together. Empower us, Lord to share what we have received. In the name of the Lord of life. Amen.

A common practice where two or three or more gather.

Walking Companions

"Now as they were eating, Jesus took bread, and blessed it, and broke it, and gave it to his disciples and said, 'Take, eat; this is my body.'" – Matthew 26:26 (RSV)

These walking companions are a real delight. They seem to be constantly present with us. These beachcombers bring joy and pleasure to those who back off, give them space, watch and listen. Often they hop about on one leg with great agility. When that second leg comes down they move into a higher gear. Their tiny little legs almost become invisible, as they shift into that highest gear. They will not disturb you and they may truly bless you. I have found them to be wonderful companions.

From time to time, listen carefully and you will hear a little "peep." As they run along the beach, they utter those soft piping notes. They received their name from those sounds. These beachcombers are sandpipers. There are over 75 species of sandpipers. These combers belong to the family called least sandpipers, or *Erolia minutilla*. These beautiful companions are just a little larger than a sparrow.

Watch their little beaks rapidly moving up and down, up and down. They are constantly searching for food and nourishment at the water's edge. It is a sight to behold. They entertain without being pushy. Again, give them a little space. Watch, listen and enjoy.

These companions remind us of our need for food and nourishment. Without food, we perish. You and I are taught that we need food, so that we will not perish. Remember the Lord's words. "Do not labor for the food which perishes, but for the food which endures to eternal life, which the Son of man will give you…." "Now as they were eating, Jesus took bread, and blessed it, and broke it, and gave it to his disciples and…."

Lord God, thank you for walking companions throughout our lives, who reminded and remind us of our own need for food that does not perish. Thank you for that need within our soul and spirit. Jesus, thank you for taking the bread and breaking it with compassion and love. Thank you for giving. Father, give us grace and power to share, with love, the need for food that will not perish. In the name of the one we are taught to call "The Bread of Life." Amen.

Remember: never alone.

Keep eyes and spiritual eyes open for the companion.

Kayak Tours

"So Phillip ran to him, and heard him reading from Isaiah the prophet, and asked, 'Do you understand what you are reading?' And he said, 'How can I, unless someone guides me?' " – Acts 8:29-30 (RSV)

It happens several times a week in the summer at Gould's Inlet, East Beach. The kayak tour guides arrive early, with kayaks and with the necessary equipment in hand for a truly treasured adventure in the marsh and the tidal creeks of Glynn. The kayaks are placed neatly side by side, next to the water. Everyone selects and stands by his or her kayak. First timers are usually the most eager for guidance and direction. The tour guide begins with the life jacket, making sure that it has been properly secured. Safety is number one. Next comes guidance on how to use the carefully designed paddle. Next comes the kayak itself, its design, capability and rudder control. There are instructions about staying close in and even instructions in how to exit the Kayak quickly, if it becomes necessary. By the way, one of the guides leads the tour and another brings up the rear. All are in the water and in this adventure together!

We need guides. I am writing this and you are reading this, because somewhere along the way, we were eager for a guide, for guidance, for direction and God provided. We were like those first timers on East Beach. Can you name one of your early guides? Can you remember times, when you were very eager? I can. Most of us can. "How can I, unless someone guides me?" We give thanks for prayers, for the Bible, for the Spirit, but also for flesh and blood...a

183

human being. We needed someone who was willing and who understood. There is great joy and peace and love, when someone cares enough about us to simply listen and to wait with kindness. We never outgrow that need. Again, there is joy, peace and love, when someone gets in the water with us.

The exciting beautiful news is this; we are freely, lovingly, tenderly invited to be guides ourselves. "Love God and love your neighbor!" "Let your light so shine." Remember what has been given and what has been received and join the team. Care, listen, wait, love, give and yes, get in the water yourself. There is a deep and abiding joy in being a guide. Dear Lord may it be so!

Loving Father, thank you for guides. Thank you for those you provide for us. Lord, may we honor you and honor them. In His precious name. Amen.

Kayaks prepared. *Original Photograph by Diane Corbitt*

Feeding Grounds

"Blessed are those who hunger and thirst for righteousness, for they will be filled." – Matthew 5:6 (NIV)

Ibises were feasting on the riches from Bloody Marsh. The marshes are wonderful feeding grounds for many of God's creatures: great blue herons, egrets, whimbrels, fish, turtles, shrimp, crabs, raccoons, rabbits, spiders, and the list goes on. The insect population is very large.

We human beings need feeding grounds as well. Army helicopter pilots visit McKinnon airport on St. Simons Island regularly. They come from the Savannah area. They need to practice flying, navigating, landing, take offs and other skills. In the in between time of landing and taking off, they have found a great feeding ground at Southern Soul Barbeque, not far from the airport. It needs to be said that, St. Simons is famous for feeding grounds. Personally, Sweet Mama's and the Frederica House are tops on my list. When one of our daughters comes to visit, one of her first priorities is to get to Sweet Mama's the next morning and hopefully be the first one there.

We need feeding grounds.

"Blessed are those who hunger and thirst for righteousness, for they will be filled." We need to hunger and thirst for righteousness, (right living in God's sight)! When we do that with heart, with soul and with mind, we will be filled! That's the truth. That's His promise.

How do we do that? It begins with a choice and the answer comes only by grace. It begins with that first small step... saying yes. At that moment, hunger for right living in God's sight begins.

How do we feed that hunger? Where do we go for spiritual food? Go to those people who encourage that hunger and thirst in you. Ask them, how they do it.

Lord God, thank you for that need in each of us for spiritual food. Thank you for those you have sent our way to help us recognize that need within. Thank you for filling our lives with the fruit of right living; love, joy, peace, patience, kindness, goodness, faithfulness, gentleness, and self-control. In His holy name. Amen.

Needed: Feeding grounds.

A Feather

"And God said, 'Let the water teem with living creatures, and let birds fly above the earth across the expanse of the sky.' So God created the great creatures of the sea and every living and moving thing with which the water teems, according to their kinds, and every winged bird according to its kind. And God saw that it was good."
– Genesis1:20-21 (NIV)

It was a seagull's feather. Often they are found on the beach. There are those who see a feather as a treasure. I feel that way. Focus on the next one you see. A feather is so very delicate and so amazing. It is magnificently and beautifully designed, surely no accident of nature. A feather is ultra-light, very smooth to a gentle touch. A feather is very strong and very fragile. Handle with care!

Feathers are designed for flight, but not alone. They must be joined with other feathers to make flight a reality. Together with the wings, they lift the body with ease and soar "above the earth across the expanse of the sky." It is indeed a sight to behold, yet so easily missed.

Paul lovingly reminds his brothers and sisters in Corinth, "The eye cannot say to the hand, 'I don't need you.' And the head cannot say to feet, 'I don't need you.' " There is one body, but many parts. Like the feather alone, it will never soar, but with the other parts, they will soar together!

We, you and I, have been carefully designed by God, our Father to be a very important part of the Body of Christ.

No one takes our place. There is an empty space, when we are not present spiritually. We are designed to love, to care, to serve, to give, to live abundantly. Remember Paul. "So faith, hope, love abide, these three. But the greatest of these is love." Yes, we are indeed designed to soar. When we honor Him together, glory is given and received. Yes, indeed we soar.

Keep your eye out for a feather. Put it on your desk, or place where you see it often and remember to soar. But even more importantly, remember together!

Dear Lord, thank you for the birds of the air. Father, remind us that we are a part of the Body of Christ and none of us are insignificant in your sight. Empower us to love and to soar together and give glory and honor to you, day by day. In His holy name. Amen.

A Feather from the white sand.

Hope

"We have this hope as an anchor of the soul, firm and secure. It enters the inner sanctuary behind the curtain, where Jesus, who went before us, has entered on our behalf." – Hebrews 6:19-20a (NIV)

This was the last devotional written for this book. It has been a beautiful venture, a valued discipline and a spiritual eye opener.

I began the exercise shortly after arriving on the beach. I offered the spiritual eye within. I lifted the prayer that has become a lifetime gateway, "Lord, I am looking and I am listening." Often it takes time and sometimes it doesn't occur on that particular outing, but on this day it happened almost instantly.

What I saw was hope! There were two little girls...probably second or third graders with a wet and sandy football. They were about fifteen to twenty feet apart. One threw the ball to her friend...totally missing her. Her friend ran and picked it up and threw it back...again, totally missing her. This continued on as I slowly walked by. Each time that ball was thrown, I saw hope and I joined in that precious hope for them. This time will be the one when the ball is thrown and caught...oh, the joy of that moment. Remember that hope within, that precious gift...that joy divine.

The Psalms echoes the theme of hope..."hope in the Lord." "Be strong and take heart, all you who hope in the Lord." (Psalm 31:24) "O Israel, put your hope in the Lord."

(Psalm 130:7) "But now, Lord, what do I look for? My hope is in you." (Psalm 39:7) "Why, my soul, are you downcast? Why so disturbed within me? Put your hope in God, for I will yet praise Him, my Savior and my God." (Psalm 42:5)

Paul puts it very clearly, "So faith, hope, love abide..." Faith and hope are producers of love and joy and peace. He adds "May the God of hope fill you with all joy and peace." The writer of Hebrews makes it clear, "We have this hope as an anchor of the soul, firm and secure."

Lord God, Father, thank you for the holy gift of hope. Thank you for two little girls exercising hope on the beach. Lord Jesus, we thank you for those who with love and faith taught us to exercise our faith and our hope in you...may we encourage others in faith and hope. In the name of Jesus Christ. Amen.

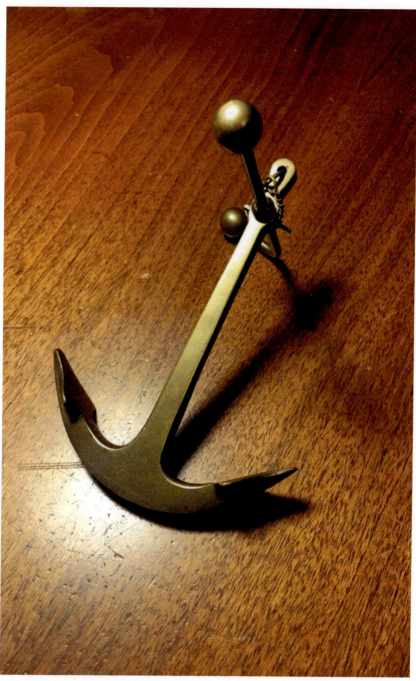

An anchor of the soul.

Beyond

"But thanks be to God, who gives us the victory through our Lord Jesus Christ." – I Corinthians 15:57 (RSV)

As I sat on the bench, with the marsh and the sunset before me, I saw beyond! I had just completed my last visit with my friend, Luanne. I knew she would never sit on this bench again, or see another sunset. We had been friends for many years. The truth was we were more than friends. We were laborers together in His vineyard. She was a wonderful caregiver. I had learned a great deal from her. That "laboring together" created a holy and sacred bond.

She had waged war with cancer for several years. Luanne had kept the faith and had fought the good fight. By the grace of our faithful Father, she had received the victory. I am confident she had heard those precious words..."Enter into the joy of your master..." She was indeed prepared!

Back to the bench. She loved to ride her bike and sit on this bench...the marsh and sunset before her. After our last visit, I was led by what I understand to be the Spirit of the living Lord to ride my bike, to sit on her bench, and to wait, watch and listen. I waited. I watched. I listened.

Sunsets are normally closure times. We come to the close of another day. Not so for me on this day...I truly saw beyond. The marsh was at its very best. The sunset was glorious. It was indeed another God-given kaleidoscope... reds, yellows, pinks, oranges, roses, violets, blues, etc. Pick your best sunset and multiply.

Shortly after the sun dipped beyond the horizon, I saw a multitude of jet streams. They were completely invisible just a second before. The sheltering earth and the new angle of the sunlight illuminated them. Then I felt a gentle breeze. The airliners were filled with those on their own spiritual pilgrimages. I wondered where they were headed. At that moment, in my spirit and in my soul, again I saw beyond. I thought of Luanne and others, family and friends, who had completed their earthly pilgrimage and had received the Victor's Crown. Tears of joy filled my spirit. My soul soared far beyond the jet streams.

About ten hours after my visit to Luanne's bench, a little before sunrise, she crossed over, went beyond, to that place not made with human hands, but eternal in the heavens.

Father, we thank you. We thank you for your Son. We thank you for your Holy Spirit and for the hope that burns within our souls. We thank you for the gift of life and for those who, with love and care point us toward you. We thank you for the victor's crown and for the home not made with human hands, but eternal. Empower us to share the hope and faith you have so generously given us. In the name of the victor, Jesus Christ. Amen.

The Frederica River, the pier at Epworth by the Sea.

Photographs by the Sea

And God said, "Let the water teem with living creatures, and let birds fly above the earth across the expanse of the sky." So God created the great creatures of the sea and every living and moving thing with which the water teems, according to their kinds, and every winged bird according to its kind. And God saw that it was good.
— Genesis 1:20 (NIV)

Sundown Comes Slowly
Bloody Marsh

Evening
Village Pier

Closing of Another Day
Epworth by the Sea/Frederica River

Sunrise
King and Prince

Celebrating the gift of Color
Village Pier

Taking flight
Bloody Marsh

In Flight
Bloody Marsh

Harmony

Focus

Watching the tide go out
Mackay River

Closing out the day with pink clouds

A Gift from God
East Beach

More feeding ground
East Beach

Nesting by the Sea
East Beach

Beauty in Flight
*Original Photograph
by Carol Conner*

In unison
East Beach

Traveling together early in the morning
King and Prince

October sunrise
Goulds Inlet

Made in the USA
Lexington, KY
01 February 2018